The Art of SalesFu

10 Steps to Selling Anything Over the Phone

SUNDANCE BRENNAN

A Sales Nerds Book

How Strong is your SalesFu?

The Sales Nerds
PO BOX 198900
PMB 214
Hawi, HI 96719
www.thesalesnerds.com

This book is dedicated to the most important sale of my life- my wonderful wife.

I love you.

This is also dedicated to the best salespeople I've ever met- my kids. They are relentless when closing the deal. They never take no for an answer and even when they do hear rejection, they seem to instantly forget it.

-    *Sundance Brennan*

TABLE OF CONTENTS

SalesFu Introduction

It dawned on me recently that I've been practicing the art of sales and perfecting my sales style for over 20 years now. I've sold everything from household goods via living room presentations, to wedding packages over the phone. I like the face to face interaction, but my favorite type of sales interaction is over the phone. I'm good at it. I'm very good at it. I've sold Hawaiian music CD's, minivans, taxicabs, vacation deals, and mortgages all over the phone and internet. I've worked in call centers for the better part of the last decade and I've opened several offices for very large employers. Every job site has the same problem, though - Retention.

I've probably seen 1500 sales agents come in one door and then go out another. Why do so many people have a hard time in the sales industry? They clearly knew what they were getting into, and then suddenly decided that they couldn't make it work, or worse yet, the decision was made for them by upper management. One young lady actually said, "I didn't realize I was going to be on the phone that much." How does this happen in a call center? Isn't that part of the job description?

There are comprehensive training programs out there, and there are more sales books than I care to read. There are great sales speakers and online videos to watch of the greats like Ziglar, Tracy, and Hopkins but those guys and all the other guys I've seen with programs to pitch and memberships to sell, have some crazy magnetic charm. They have some swarthy gene that I just wasn't born with. I'm a natural introvert. That's right, I'm an introvert. Honestly, I'm scared of talking to people. I'd be more comfortable at home reading a book or playing a video game.

I have however learned to crave the uncomfortable, so I've forced myself to study sales. I've had to dissect it and learn the psychological nuances and reasons that make people say yes. I've had to devise techniques that I've originally stolen, modified, and personalized over the years to make work. I refuse to sound like the salesman's salesman as I've heard in the industry. What many think of as the "Used Car Salesman", pitch and close technique just isn't my gig. We all know about the pushy sales rep that won't go away and keeps pushing until you either meekly say yes or slither away. The problem with that sales technique is that it works. The pushy sales rep will get a yes or a no from every customer and a certain percentage will say yes. It's a numbers game, it doesn't matter how many times a salesperson hears, "No", what matters is how many times they heard, "Yes". So, the pushy sales rep lives to see another day and that style is encouraged because it works.

I've got a better way though; I've got a secret. Nothing in this book is totally new. Nothing in this book should be earth-shattering. The truth is that any system works, at least a certain percentage of the time, SalesFu just has better percentages. Like most salespeople, I've taken the best of what I've learned from others and made it my own. I've taken theories I first saw in women's studies, communication, sociology, and psychology classes in the '90s and combined it with a thoughtful guiding approach that works for training new hires and for guiding new customers through a tough purchase process. I've taken ideas and techniques and molded them together into one sales philosophy for the modern era. We don't need sales gorillas willing to beat their chest for a deal, we need sales professionals who don't insult intelligence and bully customers into a sale. We need salespeople who will proactively guide and influence a customer until what the customer wants and what we want are the same. There is no doubt that we must first educate ourselves and then our customers before sales nirvana can be reached. If you want a career in sales and you want to do it ethically so you can sleep well at night, I offer you the chance to educate yourself starting today.

I present to you – The Art of SalesFu.

SalesFu – /seylz-foo/

noun. The Art of Identifying & Capturing Customer Energy to be used in Persuading & Influencing a Purchase Decision.

~Sundance Brennan 2014

Part I ... The Green Belt

Becoming Aware of SalesFu

Hello, Greenie. The first 3 steps to becoming a SalesFu Phone Sales Master are all about mindset. If you are a seasoned pro and think your mindset is strong, go ahead and skip this part, but you'll probably regret it and come back to this section later. You must conclude that there must be a better way to sell on your own. I can't force that choice. I can't make you believe that being genuine is better than telling a customer what you think they want to hear. I can't make you believe that at their highest levels Sales and great Customer Service are indeed the same things unless you've seen it.

Every journey has a beginning and at some point, in time, we've all realized that our journeys have started with ignorance. Ignorance could be bliss, but in sales, that ignorance could cost you your career. 20 years ago, I didn't know what I didn't know and my sales sucked. Luckily it didn't stop me from getting better.

STEP 1 ... Fail – But Be Relentless

I've failed at many things in my life, both personally and professionally. I'm on my 3rd marriage. I've been about a hair's breadth from bankruptcy several times. I've been part of businesses that have gone belly up. I've lost more deals than the combined audience experiences of Monty Hall's "Let's Make a Deal" game show, and still, I move forward.

I strongly believe that we have to take our failures, and turn them into our success stories. We have to turn our greatest weaknesses into strengths. We wouldn't have any idea what success is unless we could compare it to a loss. It's important to fail, and I would argue that it's important to fail in abundance.

In 1997 I was involved in a popular Multi-Level Marketing company, I believe MLM actually had a pretty bad name at the time, (probably still does) and this company called themselves a "Network Marketing" company, but in either case I was selling vitamins, cleaning supplies, makeup, and groceries from a catalog. In the late '90s, there was a minor online presence but the business was all still grown primarily with presentations done in someone's home. I literally scheduled appointments to meet with friends and family in their living rooms with a giant flip chart and some samples of the various products.

I would present these friends and friends of friends with the opportunity to shop through the catalog to obtain higher quality products, in bulk orders or condensed formats and because the company I represented got to save all the marketing dollars, (based only on word of mouth sales), the company would pay us what they would have paid in marketing bills. My closing line was something like, *"Wouldn't it be great to get paid to do your normal grocery shopping from now on?"* If the customer said yes, I'd break out the pens and then ask for referrals and see if they thought they could do what I just did. If so, they could supplement their income and not only get paid to go grocery shopping, but all their groceries could be essentially free. Most people didn't say yes, or they did but wanted time to think about it or wanted to sign up when they had more money or their current supplies ran out. I was fine with that, I'm not sure why, but I was just glad to get the presentation over and not blow it. I didn't realize I had indeed already blown it.

On one pivotal day, I was in a living room and I had given my presentation and asked my question. The owner of the home said that she liked shopping at the grocery store as it was like a social hour for her. She ran into the ladies there and besides; she liked Alex the Greek butcher and didn't want to put him out of a job. What if everyone started buying groceries through the mail? Wouldn't the world be a boring place, everyone sitting at home waiting around for the postman so that they could eat? She said that without a doubt this was the most horrible idea she had ever seen. I froze. I swallowed. I didn't know what to do. I think I mumbled something about it not being for everyone and then I didn't know what else to do so I asked to use her restroom.

I hid in the bathroom ladies and gentlemen.

It wasn't even a nice bathroom. It was riddled with bright pink fuzzy things, lime green walls, and a sign that said, *"If it's yellow it's mellow if it's brown flush it down."* The place also reeked of Avon. I was sure the Avon Lady had sabotaged me.

When I think back, I'm not even really sure what Avon smelled like, and I certainly don't think the Avon Lady actually had anything to do with my lousy sales skills. It turns out that I actually knew Alex the Greek butcher and I thought he was a great guy too, but I didn't even offer meat products through that company so why would my non-customer stop going to see him? Ah… hindsight is 20/20.

I do remember the feeling, though. I remember feeling helpless. I remember thinking that this was no way to earn a living. I had a horrible product; a horrible service and I must have been tricking my friends and family into buying these things at inflated prices for my own gain. They probably all hated me. I had to find something else to do and I needed to find it now. As I was washing my hands and running my fingers through my hair, waiting for an appropriate amount of time to head back out to the room, I was planning my escape. I'd go out there and be very polite and pack up my belongings and maybe I could still get a pity sale out of her, maybe she'd place a single order – Wait! Was I still thinking about trying to get a sale out of this poor old woman who clearly didn't want my products? Crap. I guess I was. Ok, I'm probably going to Hell.

I didn't get a pity sale. I should have recruited Alex the Butcher to be in my downstream, though. He could have sold anything in that living room. In fact, I'm pretty sure he started selling green algae stuff a few months later. Good for him.

I did drive home in a beat-up Kia and I came to a couple of realizations. First, I sucked as a salesperson. I had absolutely zero game. Second, I'd fix it. I was too stubborn to give up. Third, I didn't even know where to begin.

I didn't have this book to look to. I had a library card, an AOL account, and a couple of friends who were marginally more successful than I was. I went to work.

The results of that initial dive into the sales process lead to the beginnings of SalesFu. I listened to grainy audio tapes, I watched equally grainy VHS tapes, and I borrowed books that I never gave back. It wasn't the last time I failed, but it was the first time that I came back with a plan.

Failure isn't just losing. Failure is a chance to improve. Failure is what you have to measure yourself against and failure is necessary for success.

Yin and Yang.

Night and Day.

Good and Evil.

Failure and Success.

One is nothing without the other.

If you haven't failed, then you are kidding yourself. You've failed or are failing now. What's different is that you didn't blame outside sources, you didn't give reasons why your failure was the fault of someone other than yourself. You picked up this book because you didn't like the feeling, and want to avoid it in the future.

In life we can run towards the rewards or we can run from the pain. I've painted a lot of pretty pictures and offered lots and lots of rewards over the years, but the truth is that nothing motivates quite like fear. I now have a healthy fear of failure. You and I now share this fear and it's OK. It's not to say that we haven't learned anything or that the experience wasn't valuable and it's not to say that we won't take risks in the future. Fear of failure is normal, healthy and if it's harnessed properly it can help propel us to success.

SalesFu is the art of identifying & capturing customer energy to be used in persuading & influencing a purchase decision.

Before we can do that, though, we have to identify and capture our own energy so we can redirect it to a positive place.

Think about your own failures. What has driven you to this point right now? What will you be willing to do to avoid that failure again in the future? Will you read this book? Will you be disciplined in your approach? Will you be relentless in your pursuit of becoming better? Will you dare to do more? Will you dare to think more? Will you dare to act more, ask more, work more, and get up again tomorrow to do it all over again?

No one steps into The Dojo without some battle scars.

STEP 2 … Get up Again- 5 Moves to Impose Your Will

In sales, we need to know what it is to fail. In life, we need to know that we always have to get up again. There is no choice. A few quotes come to mind.

"Whether you think you can, or you think you can't – you're right." – Henry Ford.

"It does not matter how many times you get knocked down, but how many times you get up." – Vince Lombardi

Failure is the precursor to great success. The person that stays within their comfort zone and always remains "safe" is not the person that will reach for success. That safe person just wants to remain average and under the radar. The safe salesman waits until the customer asks, "*So what do we do next?*" before actually asking for the business. The safe zone means that there is very little chance of failure and very little chance that feelings get hurt. There is also very little chance that anything besides a mediocre paycheck gets deposited.

Safe sucks. I've seen safe salespeople keep their heads above water for a few years, but inevitably something unplanned happens and they aren't prepared. They aren't prepared for massive action and their safe approach just doesn't cut it. They get sick or some 3rd party or event interferes with the company production and that safe approach is suddenly the underperforming approach. We all know what happens to underperforming safe salespeople. It's safe to say they find themselves in horrible situations and usually, blame someone or something else for their predicament because they did everything right, they played it safe for crying out loud.

I've hedged a few bets in my day and I've bought insurance from the dealer a time or two. It didn't really do me any good, though. I might have lost a little less, but I certainly didn't win any more. The falling down isn't really what hurts, that's usually pretty easy. The hard part is actually getting back up and still be willing to risk it all to do the right thing.

I've heard this philosophy called –

Law of Attraction

Manifest Destiny

Positive Thinking

And Making your own Luck

I just call it getting what you want. You must learn to **Impose Your Will** on the world. The world doesn't owe you anything, but that doesn't mean you can't take it. Here are my 5 moves designed to help you Impose Your Will on the world.

MOVE #1

Don't be a Victim

You can't impose your will if you are at the whim of someone else's. The sad thing is that most Victims don't really understand that they are the victim by choice. We are talking about people who are always subject to their surroundings, circumstances, bad luck, and general voodoo. People like this don't take control of their current situation, let alone their future.

I know some very nice Victims. I just don't like to be around them when something goes wrong and it is definitely, positively, absolutely never ever their fault. In fact, life is entirely unfair and they are bombarded by issues outside of their control. It's easy to identify a Victim- they are the ones with excuses and endless apologies. I don't mean to be too harsh here. I know that it takes all types of people to create a balanced world. I also know that everyone I know that has had some success did it because they saw the opportunities in the world, they didn't see the roadblocks. The

Victims of the world see the glass as half empty, and someone stole that first half anyway.

To break out of the Victim mentality we have to force ourselves to be relentlessly positive. I'm talking RELENTLESSLY positive. It takes some time to force the goodwill out of every situation. It takes practice to see the benefit of every action or event. It takes some serious discipline to see the positive in everyone. Being positive doesn't automatically remove you from the Victim category, but at least you aren't blaming anyone. Blame implies that something went wrong and someone or something needs to take responsibility. Being positive removes the negative aspect, now there isn't a situation that requires "Blame."

When something goes wrong are you worried that people will blame you? When there is an issue do you look for someone or something to blame it on? We tell ourselves that it's important to find the cause of the issue, that's why we level blame. Who is to blame? Is it you? If you feel the need to avoid or redirect blame, you are a Victim.

Instead of finding the blame or directing the blame, just find a solution. I have to tell you; I've seen some awful stuff happen. So, have you, but you know what? You are still here. There is nothing besides actual death that is so bad we can't overcome it. Everything in your past has come to pass and it's turned out OK. It might not have been fun, but you are a better person with more experiences and you are still moving forward. Time heals. Look for the silver lining in the situation and move on.

Just because I choose to see the glass as half full doesn't mean I don't take responsibility for my actions. We all have to take FULL responsibility for our results. We can only control what we can control. The Victim gives up that control though and just lets life happen. No wonder the Victim feels so helpless and lost- they are just adrift in the world. I choose to control everything and whatever I can. I'm not a control freak, but if I'm given the choice between controlling my destiny and just living someone else's dream, I choose to control my destiny.

I even choose to control accidents. At a fine dining restaurant in San Francisco, a waiter spilled red wine on me. Too many people would say that the waiter should lose his job or the staff should be better trained. Instead, I look at what I could have done to avoid the situation. I could have sat on the other side of the table. I could have moved my glass a little closer to the edge of the table. I could have noticed that the restaurant was too busy and too crowded for the staff to pour the wine comfortably. I could have ordered a cocktail. Come to think of it, I don't wear white dress shirts to restaurants anymore. I wear dark colors whenever possible when dining out now; it's what I can control.

There are actions we can each take to limit our risk in the world. When we do take those calculated risks and wear white to the restaurant, we know it's because we think we look really good in that shirt or dress and it's worth the risk. If we get food or wine spilled on it, that's the risk we took. Is it someone's fault? Do we really need to sign a waiver to eat? Do we need to acknowledge that the coffee is "really" hot? Is it someone else's fault if you find a fingertip in a can of chili? You know there is some nasty stuff in canned food, right? Just think about the guy that lost his finger, he deserves the $100,000 legal settlement, not you. You just need another can of chili, or stop eating that stuff and visit the farmers market.

Find the good. Ignore the blame.

Take responsibility. Take action.

MOVE #2

Find Strength in Weakness

Part of being positive is always finding the silver lining, looking on the bright side, and being hopelessly optimistic. This doesn't mean you have your head in the sand. Just because I see failure as an opportunity to learn and I'm thankful, doesn't mean that I don't take action to correct the situation. We are all responsible for our future. We owe it to our future selves, to our children, to the next generation to learn from our mistakes. We can all be better tomorrow than we are today.

I choose to identify my weaknesses and make them my strengths. At first, I didn't really know that I was socially awkward. I had an idea, but I assumed everyone was like me. You know what happens when you assume right? It turns out that about 90% of the population is more outgoing than I am. With a current population of about 7 billion, though, that also means that

I'm more outgoing than about 700,000 people. That seems doesn't seem so bad, does it? It's not bad unless you've chosen a profession that depends on your ability to relate to people and earn their trust. It means that 90% of the people I speak with have a different set of norms and a different way of communicating. 20 years ago, I didn't know most people have their own communication style. I spoke how I would want to be spoken to and I got through to less than 10% of the prospects I was in contact with. I was a communication failure.

Fast forward 20 years and I make my living communicating and teaching others to do the same. I can do this because most people take their communication skills for granted. Most people get by just fine without studying communication techniques. Most people are oblivious that communication styles even exist and that they are different for different people. As you will see in later Steps, I use personality types and communication styles extensively to thrive in the sales world. I took my weakness and made it my strength. I Imposed my Will and took control of my weakness before someone else could.

Truth be told, it wasn't that hard. It took practice, time, dedication, and diligence but it wasn't physically taxing. It probably wasn't harder than learning another spoken language. It did take about 10,000 hours of speaking on the phone, listening to conversations, reading books, giving speeches, and watching the interactions of others before I could safely say that I knew more than most people. Now, 10,000 hours of communication may seem like a lot but it's only about 4 years. You spend at least 7 hours a day with other human beings, right? The difference is that I had to go home and write down those interactions, gauge responses, ask for feedback, and try to communicate ideas again in different ways to test my theories. As a result, I now know more about how you interact and communicate than you do.

Have you heard of visually impaired people who develop their other senses? Some blind people can get around just fine without a cane. Most have a higher appreciation for sounds, tastes, smells, and tactile sensations than the average person with 20/20 vision. I have seen amazing artists who are blind. I've seen a tattoo artist with no arms. I've seen tone-deaf musicians and we've all seen the bald barber! So, I'm socially blind. What is your Achilles heel?

Identify your weakness before someone else does.

Work on it until it's your Strength.

MOVE #3

<u>Redirect Energy</u>

There is no way to 100% eliminate negative energy. The trick is to take that energy and redirect it to someplace positive. In terms of Imposing your Will, this means that we need to direct that energy where we want so that our goal is still obtained.

When we are talking about energy here, we are talking about someone else's will power or a group's demeanor. When someone is confrontational it's often our impulse to meet that confrontation head-on, to not back down. This can result in an argument or at the least an agreement to disagree. This kind of confrontation does nothing to resolve the situation. Someone gets their way but rarely is the losing party on board with the decision. The head to head combat approach produces a winner and a loser, but typically no one's opinion is truly changed.

If you want to impose your will on the world or at least a particular situation on a particular day, you need to persuade others to help you. I didn't say "Coerce" or "Strong Arm" your way to that help, I said "Persuade". The difference is that someone who is persuaded goes along willingly.

Step 2 of SalesFu is all about what to do after a failure, in many cases, we've been pushed down, aside, or out of the way. When we get up it's time to Catch the Wave or Set the Sail, some force just overwhelmed us and there are forces of character everywhere. A sailor will tell you that sometimes it's best to catch a current, but even if the current is against you, it's still possible to move by setting the sail and harnessing the wind, we all have rudders that can help us steer. As SalesFu masters, we need to identify the various forces available to us and to use those forces to get to where and what we want.

It's easier than you think and most Gurus call this positive thinking or some kind of self-manifested goal-reaching. The thought is that if you are relentlessly positive and you assume that everyone and everything is there to help you on your way to obtaining your goals, then you will see every opportunity to hitch a ride to your ultimate destination. You will unconsciously redirect the energy of those around you because you assume, they are there to help you anyway.

This works just as well when you consciously control your surroundings. It's called Persuasion. Often our journeys are completed by hitching our wagon to one personality or idea, it's more like hitchhiking, you know where you want to go and you'll get there one way or the other but most of the time someone else is helping you. Let's say you are hungry but don't have a car. You ask your friend to pick you up and take you to a restaurant and either wait around or come back to get you. That doesn't sound like much fun for your friend and even if you get a ride today, I bet you don't get another one in the future. Your friends would stop answering your calls with this type of request. If, however, you called your friend and started a conversation about what they were doing today followed by a question about what their favorite food was, you'd have a decent shot at getting them to come to pick you up and take you out to eat.

So, what if your car broke down or the restaurant close to your house closed up, don't let life dictate what happens. Impose your Will on the world by redirecting energy to get what you desire. The trick is to always be looking to harness momentum. Your friend already had momentum going, they were going to live today no matter if you called and started talking about food or not. They were going to be eating today, whether you called or not. You just took their momentum and asked them to share it with you.

In the sales world, it's easy to get a customer to say "NO." Just ask the wrong question and all momentum stops. What you do after this will make or break your early career. Typically, a customer will tell you what they want, or at least what they think they want. Imagine this exchange-

Customer: "I want to buy a Purple Car today."

Greenie: "I'm sorry sir, all I have are Red and Green cars today, would you like to look at those?"

Customer: "Nope, I'm on a mission for a Purple Car. See you later."

That customer had momentum that was going to bring him together with a purple car! The Greenie Sales Rep was defeated when asked about a product he didn't offer. He asked a question that seems logical, he offered an alternative. Sales isn't about logic, though, it's all about emotion. Be careful with emotion though or you could end up with this exchange-

Customer: "I want to buy a Purple Car today."

Greenie: "A Purple Car? Come on, no one buys a Purple Car. The last Purple Car I saw was in a parade and there were clowns in it! Let me show you some real cars."

Customer: "Um, no. You weren't listening to me. I said I'm looking for a Purple Car and I need a Purple Car. I'm going somewhere where they won't waste my time."

That customer had momentum, and the Greenie Sales Rep was defeated when asked about a product he didn't have. Instead of taking the SalesFu approach to redirect the energy, the approach was to use emotion to shame the customer into moving forward with something else. This approach seldom works and when it does it takes up way too much energy to spend on that one sale. When you approach the conversation or sales in general like it's a boxing match and you need to beat your opponent into submission you are creating double the work for yourself. Not only did you have to spend time halting all momentum that the customer had, but you will also need to spend time and energy building up that momentum in an entirely new direction. Instead, imagine this exchange-

Customer: "I want to buy a Purple Car today."

SalesFu Master: "Great! We've got a ton of new products to jump into today. Let's start by looking at the actual vehicles and determine which model is best for you to move forward with."

Customer: "Perfect, I was thinking about a VW Bug, a Mini Cooper, or maybe a Fiat. My friends and I are clowns in a traveling circus and if I buy it for the show it's a tax write-off."

Suddenly it all makes sense now. When a customer asks for a product you don't have or gives an objection to making a purchase right then and there it isn't your job to halt the process until you convince them to move forward. When you do that, the customer is forced to defend their position and thus becomes fully entrenched into that choice. You made it tougher for them to change their mind by forcing them to think of reasons to justify their choice. In today's world where the telephone has replaced face to face sales, it's pretty easy for a prospect to just hang up the phone.

Stay hopelessly optimistic. Don't fight it, write it.

Say YES before NO.

MOVE #4

<u>Show True Grit</u>

I like my salespeople a little Gritty. Failure provides an opportunity to grow and learn, but to take advantage of that opportunity you need True Grit. I don't know exactly how to grow True Grit; I only know how to identify it. I know it when I see it.

I know that in order to impose your will on the world you must be resilient. I know that you must fail and have the fortitude to get up again and carry on with whatever it takes to obtain your goals. I know that everyone faces a test when you fail do you have what it takes to get up again? Do you have the ability to shake off the naysayers and get through on determination alone? Have you ever been in a situation where 90% of the population would have turned back, given up, thrown their hands up in the air, but because you carried on you were able to find success?

Are you able to focus on a goal with borderline obsession? Are you willing to take unreasonable actions to obtain unreasonable results? True Grit means that you can make the sacrifices necessary to obtain a goal. Not just a short-term goal like a monthly or quarterly goal. We are talking about long-term change, habits, and success. Michael Jordan didn't become great because he practiced relentlessly for a month, a summer, a year, or even a couple of college seasons. Michael Jordan became great because he dedicated himself to his craft on and off the court. The same goes for Wayne Gretzky, Jerry Rice, Roger Federer, Tiger Woods, and all of the other sports heroes that have risen above the rest.

The comparison isn't restricted to sports, although in the sales world we often steal the terminology from great sports games to encourage competition and motivation. Think about the great leaders who have failed miserably, Abraham Lincoln ran for office at least 8 times before finally winning an election. Thomas Edison famously failed over and over again before successfully creating a light bulb that would last and be commercially viable. Donald Trump has filed for corporate bankruptcy at least four times and Steve Jobs was fired by the board at Apple before being brought back 10 years later to see great success.

The common theme here is that it takes a lifetime to gain greatness. That greatness isn't built by accident; it was built with painstaking struggle and attention to detail. Discipline and success go hand in hand. When you fail it is time to redouble your efforts, it's tougher to keep moving forward but the results will be that much more rewarding when obtained. Find a mantra or trigger to keep you going. I want to work until my Idols become my Rivals.

Be willing to take unreasonable actions to earn unreasonable rewards.

Work until your Idols become your Rivals.

MOVE #5

<u>Character and Integrity</u>

Who are you when no one is looking? What do you do? I've met people of questionable moral fiber; unfortunately, some of them have had immense wealth and success. I'm just not sure how they sleep at night. I find that it's much easier to be authentic and treat others how I'd want to be treated, or at least how they would want to be treated.

My wife just asked me about one of my morning routines. Every morning I write 4 words on the bathroom mirror with a dry erase marker – Write, Right, Health, and Wealth. These 4 words have driven me for the past year but she asked me specifically about the word, "Right" and why I feel the need to include it here. She's wondering if I need to remind myself to do the right things, shouldn't people just do the right things all the time?

Well, yes, we should do the right things all the time. It's not always easy, though. I think that people with strong Character and Integrity face the same challenges as everyone else; they just make the decisions that may not be as popular or easy but have a better long-term outcome. Should I read to my children when I get home from work or should I turn on the television and zone out with them in the same room? I think that the right thing to do is to make sure I spend time reading to them and showing the discipline to finish a longer chapter book and to help them create strong positive habits. Sometimes I still turn on the TV, though.

I believe that having good Character and Integrity is integral to being a great salesperson. True professionals help their customers and feel good about it. If your customer gets off the phone with you and instantly thinks that they just got "Sold", then you are doing something wrong. The customer believes that you are the swindler, the charlatan, the guy that says whatever is needed to get them to open up their pocketbook, you aren't authentic and your customers believe you are peddling snake oil.

Human beings aren't great lie detectors, but we know when something just doesn't feel right. You know it. I've heard salesmen say things over the phone that were blatantly false to try to earn rapport. Movies like ***Boiler Room*** and ***The Wolf of Wall Street*** make it seem like it is common practice to deceive a customer over the phone and say whatever it takes to earn a deal. I have watched both of these and I love some of the dialogue, it still gets me pumped up and excited to be a salesman today, but I know that I can only sell something I believe in.

If you want to impose your will on the world, then ultimately you need to be responsible for what you are asking for and how you accomplish your goals. Be honest with yourself, those around you, and your customers. Acknowledge your mistakes, learn from them, and take responsibility for them. When you are right, don't gloat. Just keep moving on. You don't have time for games; you've got a mission to accomplish.

Don't lie. Don't steal. Don't cheat.

Fess up when wrong and don't rub it in when you're right.

STEP 3 ... A Better Way- MORSE Code in 4 Moves.

In the last 2 steps, we have talked about failure. We may be able to spin failure into future success and learn from our mistakes, but failure still isn't fun, it's just a hurdle we have to get over. Step 3 is still focused on mindset, but it's all about the positive and finding the silver lining, sometimes creating that positivity.

I stumbled upon the MORSE Code of success in an exercise I was part of in 2006. I was with a group of future leaders and we were asked to come up with Mission, Value, and Vision statements for our sales teams. We spiraled into other topics, tangents, and sidebars, one of those sidebars lead me to think about personal success. We talked about the power of Self Talk, the need for Personal Guiding Statements, Mantra's, and how to distill those ideas into short concise messages; we talked about creating a tagline for your life.

It was a similar task often given in leadership and college classes across the world. I have been a part of a few exercises that ask you to create your obituary. In essence, what do you want to be known for after you are long gone? It's a great exercise; it could help you to determine what actions are right for you. I didn't want an obituary, though; I wanted a tagline for my life. I wanted something that would remind me of what I was going to do, not what was already done. I came up with 5 words.

Manufacture **O**pportunity. **R**ealize it. **S**hare it. **E**xecute.

MOVE #1

<u>Manufacture Opportunity</u>

If you haven't figured it out already, I'm a big fan of self-directed destiny. I want control of my life and I believe we all take control of our actions. Selling is about persuasion and influence; I believe we can take control of our actions to produce the results we are looking for. Too often I hear salespeople asking questions early on in a presentation or negotiation that will lead the customer to think about why they shouldn't do something. "Why wouldn't you want to do this?" or "How come you wouldn't want to make a move right away?" and these phrases have the opposite of the intended effect 90% of the time.

The problem with finding out what your customer's objections would be in this manner is that it forces them to think of reasons they should be telling you NO. Now 10% of the time this is a loaded question because we know the answer is negligible or we are trying to ferret out the last objection because we don't know what it is, the other 90% of the time you just shot yourself in the foot. The goal in sales is to sell something, preferably something that offers a legitimate benefit, right? Sometimes we need to think outside the box and come up with solutions to problems that customers didn't even know they had.

In cases where we need to Manufacture Opportunity, we need to identify an area that needs improvement and we need to highlight that issue in a way that the customer comes to the conclusion to ask for help. With this in mind, we need to ask questions that lead down this path. We need to ask questions that create a scenario where the customer says, "YES".

Customer: "I'm not in the market for training tablets right now."

Greenie: "Really? You've got competitors using them, why wouldn't you want to use these?"

Customer: "My competitors are wasting money; we still have binders and good old paper. It helps the staff to take notes and visualize the material besides, the cost is outrageous and the technology will be outdated in 6 months. Maybe next year come back and let me know how the tech is updated and maybe the costs will go down too. Send me an email and I'll take a look next year."

Ouch. Greenie just got shut down and it's hard to come back from such a clear decision and NO statement from the customer. Once a customer thinks about and then verbalizes several reasons to say NO, then as a matter of pride it's hard for them to switch gears. We don't want customers to become entrenched in their decisions; we want them to be fluid in their decision-making process and open to new ideas. We can help this happen by Manufacturing Opportunity. Start by always agreeing with your customer, offering some vital information that outlines your point, get positive feedback along the way, and end your statement with a question that asks for feedback that will lead to a YES answer.

Customer: "I'm not in the market for training tablets right now."

*SalesFu Master: "**Exactly, no one is**! Everyone waits until right after the big tech conventions to see what is new and exciting. What they don't know is that the market isn't releasing anything* earth-shattering this year but right before the conventions we raise prices with the new models and even after discounts you'll pay more than you would right now. Plus, the tablets come with 5 years of software upgrades now, so you'll get tomorrow's technology at today's prices anyway! ***How much did you spend on training last year, I'm not talking about new equipment, guest speakers, training staff salaries or training space, just physical hard copies and binders last year for new hires?"***

Customer: *"I don't know exactly but maybe $18 a binder, we, had about 400 new hires come through so that's a little more than $7,000 probably, we consider it a good investment."*

SalesFu Master: *"**Of course** your training material is vital to your success! Let's do some math, though; I love numbers, you too probably because the answers are always so clear. Ok, let's say your company stays the same size, which is being ultra-conservative right? But let's just say you stay at 400 new hires a year for 5 years @ $18 a binder, that's $36,000 you've committed to training right now, a good investment. However, of those 2000 new hires, only 50 get trained at a time, right? So 50 tablets will only run you $5500. Which brings me to the question- **What will you do with the other $30,500?***

Boom. Now the customer is thinking of ways to spend the extra funds you freed up and you've already planted the seeds by asking, (but not asking) about "***new equipment, guest speakers, training staff salaries or training space...***"

Keep your head on a swivel and search for opportunities, not excuses.

MOVE #2

__Realize it.__

One of the toughest things to do here is to see the opportunity. We often pass up the very opportunity we've been looking for because it didn't knock us down and beg to be taken advantage of. Think about how many opportunities you've passed up in your life because you didn't realize that they were there in the first place. The phrase "Hindsight is 20/20" is popular because so many people have missed so many opportunities.

Part of the MORSE Code is keeping an open mind and always being on the lookout for an opportunity. Keep your eyes open and your head on a swivel. Have you heard the story about the man stuck on the roof of his home during a flood? He passed up the opportunity to get on a homemade raft with a neighbor, to jump onto a rescue boat with the Coast Guard, and to get lifted out via helicopter with the National Guard, all because he thought God would save him. When the man died he met God and asked why God didn't save him. God told the man that he tried, he sent a neighbor to help, the Coast Guard and National Guard but the man kept refusing the opportunity to be saved.

Don't be the salesperson that dies out because you refuse to see the opportunity right in front of your face. When someone offers to help, maybe you should take it. Don't let your pride get in the way and don't refuse help because it didn't take the exact form that you thought it would. If you have manufactured the opportunity or just stumbled upon it, take advantage of it!

There is always a silver lining, a way to take advantage of the situation that's presented, and a way to move forward. Find it.

MOVE #3

<u>Share it.</u>

Once you have identified an opportunity don't keep it all to yourself! Others would counsel you to keep opportunities to yourself to hoard the advantage. There is an amazing atmosphere of competition in the sales world. I get it; often the guy at the bottom of the production board is the guy that gets cut. Sales is a competitive, dog eat dog world and we only eat what we kill. I also know that there is something fundamentally different that happens when we stop playing King of the Hill and start playing No Man Left Behind.

Here is what I mean- Let's say you find a way to outsmart your competition, or to work the system so that you have a slight advantage. You might make the biggest paycheck in your office. 2 years from now your company will still be going out of business though because even though you hit your goal, the company missed the target. Guess what? You are now out of work like everyone else.

Now, let's imagine that you found a better way to present your product, let's say you shared that opportunity and now all of your sales agents are more competitive and you gain market share. A crazy thing happens when you gain market share, you start to pick up that Sales MO, that momentum is now on your side. When more people are using your product or service more people WANT to use your product or service. Your company is now the leader in your niche and you are still getting the highest paycheck in the office, but now everyone is making more money. Get it?

When you make it to the top of the mountain turn around and help the next man up. It's likely you just climbed over his back to get where you are.

MOVE #4

Execute.

They say that the road to Hell is paved with good intentions. I believe that this last step is crucial to success. Without it no matter what your intentions are, you'll end up going to a dark place. Execution is the last step in the recipe, without execution, it's like making a pizza but realizing 20 minutes later that you forgot to turn the oven on. Fail.

You've stayed positive, you've Manufactured Opportunity. Then you opened your eyes and Realized what you were looking at, you then Shared what you found and now want to help others to find the same opportunity. Now, it's time to put together a plan and execute it. How will you track this opportunity? How will you systematically make sure that this doesn't slip through the cracks? How will you ensure that no matter what your team is the one that uses this opportunity to full potential?

Luckily, the system provides room for a self-fulfilling prophecy. Once you've Realized that there is an opportunity and talked about it, wrote about it, or otherwise Shared it with others, it's much harder for you to not follow through on your advice. In the example, on the previous pages, it would be easy for you to talk about selling by manufacturing the YES for training tablets but take that next step and ask someone to follow along on your sales call. Teach what you've learned to someone else, and then you'll be forced to take your advice. What's the value of good advice that no one takes?

Follow the MORSE Code of Success -

Manufacture **O**pportunity. **R**ealize it. **S**hare it. **E**xecute.

Part II ... The Blue Belt

Awareness of SalesFu takes hold

Hello, and welcome to the Blue Belt stage. In this stage, I assume that you've got your head in the right place. I assume that you are open to learning new ideas and that you not only want to get better at sales, but you've also got some idea about what your weak points are. Let's fill in the gaps for you, let's start with the definition of SalesFu.

SalesFu = The Art of Identifying & Capturing Customer Energy and using it to Persuade & Influence a Purchase Decision.

We are going to talk a lot about communication in this part of the book. We are going to learn how to read between the lines, how to say what we mean and how to use that ability to help our customers buy on Emotion, and justify that purchase with Logic. Lastly, we will learn how to control a conversation without talking more than our customers. You can guide a conversation without dominating it. This way when a customer decides to buy, it's their idea. The only people that like to be sold to are salespeople, everyone else just wants to buy from an expert.

STEP 4 ... The Personality Types.

To Capture Customer Energy, it's important to be on the same page with communication styles. This starts with identifying and mirroring the customer's personality type. There are numerous labels attached to these personality types, some involve animals and some involve different color schemes, but they all follow the same general format- How Emotional Open/Closed is the Customer and How Direct/Indirect are they about their goals? I'll quickly describe each quadrant in this chapter. To be a SalesFu Master means we must start with understanding how our customers communicate and why.

We talk about Personality Types but remember while reading this that it's not just a personality that we are selling to, it's a person.

I first came across the 4 Personality types during College in the early '90s. I was taking 8 classes at the time and working full time while still maintaining a pretty active social life. I had to be very efficient to get everything done and so I often looked for ways to cross utilize research and projects. I was actively looking for ways to make my time count for double the results but wasn't expecting this. There is something called the Baader-Meinhof Phenomenon which states that once you learn about some strange or interesting bit of information you will suddenly begin to see it everywhere.

My eyes were suddenly opened and even though it would take me years to put this information together in a way that I could use it for my Sales training, I always remembered that communication is the key to selling. To this very day when I'm looking to hire I search for and recruit communications majors, it's the closest thing to a degree in Sales that I've seen.

Use the chart below to find out what Sales Personality type you are.

What is SalesFu?

THE KEY WORDS

OPEN EMOTION

Giving	Safe	Secure	Fun	Adventure	Happy
Supportive	Trust	Family	Thrill	Excited	Dramatic
Loyal		Dependable	Action		Partnering
BOO BLUES				**RADICAL REDS**	
Helpful	Cautious	Teamwork	Positive	Different	New

*People Oriented
*Slower Friendly Pace
*Softer Tone

*Benefit Oriented
* Fast Paced Talkers
*Upbeat Attitude

INDIRECT GOALS   **DIRECT GOALS**

Analyze	Design Benefits	Logical	Dependable	Traditional	Accountable
Detail Oriented	Specific	Thorough	Results	Important	Prepared
GEEKY GREENS				**BUSINESS BROWNS**	
Reasonable		Data	Market Leader		Competitive
Precise	Recoup	Correct	ROI	Objectives	Opportunity
Fact Based	Careful	Controlled	Win/Win	Established	Responsible

* Research Oriented
*Slower Speaking
*Monotone

CLOSED EMOTIION

* Goal Oriented
*Bottom Line Speakers
*Direct and to the point- Efficient

Sales Fu = The Art of Identifying & Capturing Customer energy and using it to Persuade & Influence a purchase decision.

• • •

I ran into the Four Temperaments and the Four Humors in World Civics and Philosophy classes. I ran into the Myers-Briggs Type Indicator in my Psychology class. In my Communications class, we studied the Fundamental Interpersonal Relations Orientation. These are not all the same, but there are enough basic similarities along with dozens of other quadrant-based systems that demand attention. The idea of placing a personality type into a box and identifying how that personality communicates and views the world is as old as our written language. The origins of the Four Temperaments may come from Egypt or Mesopotamia. I was always fascinated by this separation of personalities into quadrants.

I have seen the labels changed to suit a particular need. In the Sales and Business world I've seen cool acronyms like KIND, PEAK or PACE used and I have seen the crosshair labels used to track other qualities but over the last 10 years, I have found that it's easiest and most efficient to sort using the chart I've provided.

First, you must imagine that there are colors on here. It's apparently 4 times more expensive to print a book with color, so the chances are that the chart you are looking at is in black and white. Grab a couple of colored sharpies or a couple of dry erase markers, heck grabs some crayons mark the chart up a bit. Circle "Radical Reds" in red, "Boo Blues" in blue, "Geeky Greens" in green, and "Business Browns" in brown. I'm a visual learner so the colors are really important to me. You can also go to www.thesalesnerds.com and download a copy of the chart as a pdf.

Now place a "1" below the bottom of the chart and mark "10" at the top. This next part is really important to remember. When you are in shopping mode when you are looking to buy a home, car, appliances, or whatever major purchase you might be interested in, how open are you about your emotions? 1 being Not at All and 10 being All In. 1 means you've got enough friends and you keep your cards close to your chest, just the facts. 10 means you think you need to make friends with the salesperson to get the best deal. Where do you rank yourself? Near the top or close to the bottom?

Use the chart to find out the words that will help you connect to each personality.

What is SalesFu?

THE KEY WORDS

OPEN EMOTION

Giving	Safe	Secure	Fun	Adventure	Happy
Supportive	Trust	Family	Thrill	Excited	Dramatic
Loyal		Dependable	Action		Partnering
BOO BLUES				**RADICAL REDS**	
Helpful	Cautious	Teamwork	Positive	Different	New

*People Oriented
*Slower Friendly Pace
*Softer Tone

*Benefit Oriented
* Fast Paced Talkers
*Upbeat Attitude

INDIRECT GOALS / **DIRECT GOALS**

Analyze	Design Benefits	Logical	Dependable	Traditional	Accountable
Detail Oriented	Specific	Thorough	Results	Important	Prepared
GEEKY GREENS				**BUSINESS BROWNS**	
Reasonable		Data	Market Leader		Competitive
Precise	Recoup	Correct	ROI	Objectives	Opportunity
Fact Based	Careful	Controlled	Win/Win	Established	Responsible

* Research Oriented
*Slower Speaking
*Monotone

CLOSED EMOTIION

* Goal Oriented
*Bottom Line Speakers
*Direct and to the point- Efficient

Sales Fu = The Art of Identifying & Capturing Customer energy and using it to Persuade & Influence a purchase decision.

Most salespeople will be near the top of the chart, but I suspect that most salespeople don't read as much as they should. They tend to "wing it" and get by on charisma and luck. Probably more than a few of you will register in the lower half of the scale, you are the type more likely to read to get better rather than go to a seminar or ask a friend or mentor for help. Good thing you've got this book!

Now while you are still imagining yourself in shopping mode, write a big "1" on the left of the chart, (I know it's cramped, just find the room, maybe that crayon idea wasn't the best right!?) and on the right side of the chart make another "10". Now from left to right think about how direct you are about your goals when you go shopping. People who aren't direct either don't know or won't say what their ultimate goal is. These people just tell you to make your best presentation and they will let you know if it's what they want or just have a vague idea that you might be able to help them. On the other side of the spectrum, those of you that put a 9 or a 10 in this category know exactly what it is you want when you go shopping and you voice your very specific goals. You did your research or have a very specific idea of what you want and are looking for someone to help accomplish that goal.

Have you ever met someone at a party or event and instantly the relationship just "clicked"? Have you had the opposite happen where someone just rubbed you the wrong way? Chances are that your communication styles conflicted and you were using a completely different vocabulary. Variety isn't a bad thing really, but it's hard to connect and understand someone who comes from a completely different background. In sales, we find it very easy to sell to those who are similar to ourselves but what if you are offending 75% of your prospects just with your communication style? Communication has nothing to do with your product and has very little to do with most services, yet potential clients won't even know what you are selling if you use the wrong words. The right set of KEYWORDS will increase your business by 300%.

Review the TOP RIGHT of the chart to study RADICAL REDS

What is SalesFu?

THE KEY WORDS
OPEN EMOTION

Giving	Safe	Secure	Fun	Adventure	Happy
Supportive	Trust	Family	Thrill	Excited	Dramatic
Loyal		Dependable	Action		Partnering
BOO BLUES				**RADICAL REDS**	
Helpful	Cautious	Teamwork	Positive	Different	New

*People Oriented
*Slower Friendly Pace
*Softer Tone

*Benefit Oriented
* Fast Paced Talkers
*Upbeat Attitude

INDIRECT GOALS — **DIRECT GOALS**

Analyze	Design Benefits	Logical	Dependable	Traditional	Accountable
Detail Oriented	Specific	Thorough	Results	Important	Prepared
GEEKY GREENS				**BUSINESS BROWNS**	
Reasonable		Data	Market Leader		Competitive
Precise	Recoup	Correct	ROI	Objectives	Opportunity
Fact Based	Careful	Controlled	Win/Win	Established	Responsible

* Research Oriented
*Slower Speaking
*Monotone

CLOSED EMOTIION

* Goal Oriented
*Bottom Line Speakers
*Direct and to the point- Efficient

Sales Fu = The Art of Identifying & Capturing Customer energy and using it to Persuade & Influence a purchase decision

In OPEN EMOTION & DIRECT GOALS (TOP RIGHT)–

<u>RADICAL REDS</u>

How to Identify the Radical Red - These RADICAL RED customers wear their emotions on their sleeves (**Open Emotion**) and will tell you right away what they want to accomplish (**Direct Goals**), they have nothing to hide. You will know these customers because they tend to use slang, may even curse, or use what some would consider inappropriate language. Radical Reds will introduce themselves using their first name and will want to call you by your first name. They will usually tell you right away what they want and will often challenge you to get it.

Famous Radical Reds- Jennifer Lawrence, Madonna, Robin Williams, Donald Trump, Guy Fieri, Elvis.

Tips for working with the Radical Red- These clients want to buy from someone who is a friend first, their trust system means that a friend wouldn't let them down or steer them wrong. Keep the conversation moving forward at all times and don't be afraid to incorporate humor. Be prepared to redirect the Radical Red back to the task at hand, they tend to have a lot going on and often aren't very organized. They do well if given a to-do list and then are reminded often about it. Don't make the sales process sound too scary, these folks will bolt if you make the process sounds too complicated or convoluted. Keep it very simple and very straightforward to keep their attention. The Radical Red loves to talk so you should ask a lot of questions to get them motivated to share their story. The more they talk, the more they like you. In fact, the more the Radical Red talks, the more they assume that you are just like them. This is also a trap for most Radical Red salespeople that like to talk. Radical Red salespeople typically assume that more of their customers are also Radical Red's than is accurate. We see in others what we see in ourselves and typically speak to others how we would want to be spoken to.

Key Words to use with the Radical Red-

Fun	Adventure	Happy
Thrill	Excited	Dramatic
Action	Different	Partnering
Positive	Perfect	New

Pace and Tone for the Radical Red- Pick up the pace of communication and be prepared to get sidetracked on a conversation to earn their business. If you are normally very professional, you'll need to lower your wall a little and use first names. In phone sales, we are at a disadvantage because this customer likes to press the flesh and look at his friends in the eye before spitting on his palm and shaking on it. You overcome that by picking up the pace of your conversation if you are slow-talking Radical Reds think you are talking "down" to them or that you are thinking of something untrue and it takes you a moment to come up with it. Most salespeople tend to talk too quickly and get excited naturally about their product so this isn't normally an issue.

How to Brand and Build Trust for the Radical Red- A lot of salespeople will try to build up brand recognition for the company, manufacturer, or servicer but won't spend a lot of time talking about their own personal "brand". That's a mistake with this customer. The Radical Red wants to know the company is there, but he's most concerned with you. It's a personal decision based on whether or not he likes and trusts you as a person. Use phrases that bring you to the forefront. Personally, recommend the service or product, tell a story about how you found the company, or how the product changed your life. The personal recommendation and story will sell your product way more than an email about your JD Power or BBB record.

Radical Red Summary- Keep it simple with these customers and emphasize the personal benefits of working directly with you. Be prepared to steer the conversation back to business and to share some personal information with these clients. The more personal information you share, the more likely they are to think of you as a real person and this customer buys from people, not businesses. Lower your guard and invite the customer to use your first name.

You will want them to use your first name at least 3 times before it's comfortable and familiar.

BONUS TIP – Radical Reds like to get a great deal, when it comes time to close the deal or overcome an objection you should lower your voice like it's a secret and let them know some "insider" information such as, "It's 10% off tomorrow but I'll give you the same deal today!".

Review the TOP LEFT of the chart to study BOO BLUES

What is SalesFu?

THE KEY WORDS

OPEN EMOTION					
Giving	Safe	Secure	Fun	Adventure	Happy
Supportive	Trust	Family	Thrill	Excited	Dramatic
Loyal		Dependable	Action		Partnering
BOO BLUES				**RADICAL REDS**	
Helpful	Cautious	Teamwork	Positive	Different	New
*People Oriented				*Benefit Oriented	
*Slower Friendly Pace				* Fast Paced Talkers	
*Softer Tone				*Upbeat Attitude	
INDIRECT GOALS					**DIRECT GOALS**
Analyze	Design Benefits	Logical	Dependable	Traditional	Accountable
Detail Oriented	Specific	Thorough	Results	Important	Prepared
GEEKY GREENS				**BUSINESS BROWNS**	
Reasonable		Data	Market Leader		Competitive
Precise	Recoup	Correct	ROI	Objectives	Opportunity
Fact Based	Careful	Controlled	Win/Win	Established	Responsible
* Research Oriented				* Goal Oriented	
*Slower Speaking		*CLOSED EMOTIION*		*Bottom Line Speakers	
*Monotone				*Direct and to the point- Efficient	

Sales Fu = The Art of Identifying & Capturing Customer energy and using it to Persuade & Influence a purchase decision

In OPEN EMOTION & INDIRECT GOALS (TOP LEFT)–

<u>BOO BLUES</u>

How to Identify the Boo Blue - These clients tend to share a lot of personal stories (**Open Emotion**) about family or personal issues. They usually have just a vague or maybe no idea of what their goal is (**Indirect Goals**) but they are pretty sure that they need help. BOO BLUES are named not only because they may be more open to sharing personal stories of heartbreak but also because they may be prone to being emotionally scared off. Ever have a customer tell you that your deal just didn't "Feel Right"? That was quite possibly a Boo Blue personality.

Famous Boo Blues- Oprah Winfrey, Big Bird, Kristen Stewart, Mr. Rogers, Michael Jordan, Paul McCartney.

Tips for working with the Boo Blue- These customers need to be coddled and you need to be the Sales Sheppard and lead them to safety. These clients value family and have a people-first mentality. A lot of Boo Blues have been taken advantage of in the past because they avoid confrontation and will tend to go along with a strong personality. It's easy for a Boo Blue to say Yes at the moment because they have a hard time hurting someone's feelings and saying No. This means that this is the customer that you thought was a 100% for sure lay down deal, but then they just go MIA and never pick up the phone again. This happens because the customer is scared that they will pick up the phone again and get Sold by you. They don't like your deal or someone in their family doesn't like your deal. This customer will often defer to someone else's judgment like a family member or a close friend so you'll have to get past a gatekeeper if you don't fully earn the Boo Blue's trust. Avoid open confrontation with this customer, instead use your skills to persuade and influence.

Key Words to use with the Boo Blue-

Giving	Safe	Secure
Supportive	Trust	Family
Loyal	Personally	Dependable
Helpful	Cautious	Teamwork

Pace and Tone for the Boo Blue- Slow down and take your time with this personality, these folks are loyal once they decide so it's worthwhile. There is a reason that salespeople are referred to as "Fast Talkers", it's because most salespeople have a natural tendency to pick up the pace. We are impatient and want to get to the good stuff right away! There is so much good stuff to talk about how are we going to fit it all in!? Fight the urge to spew out all of the great info and ideas you have, take a big giant breath, and pick just a few strong statements to make. Boo Blues can get put off by loudspeakers as well. Keep a lower tone that conveys a cool, calm, and collected demeanor. If you raise your voice or get excited this customer will interpret it as a threat, even if you are just super enthusiastic to help.

How to Brand and Build Trust for the Boo Blue- The Boo Blue isn't going to be impressed by your company's web page or your 100-year-old company history. They buy because of you. Talk about how the company makes changes in lives. Talk about your personal journey to find the right company, the right situation, the right people to work with for the right reasons. If you share your personal story you are vouching for the company. You did your homework and found this company and liked them so much that you were willing to attach your name to theirs with pride. After you share a personal story it's important to make your customer feel like family. Your company is like one big family and you are inviting your customer to join the family, or maybe you are asking them to invite you to be part of theirs.

Boo Blue Summary- For a Boo Blue, buying something is a very personal decision. They are people-oriented and worry about how a buying decision will impact those around them. Often, they make decisions *because* of the family. They need a new car to have reliable transportation for their family. They need to buy a new home because "Home is where the heart is" and they have a tendency to want to please everyone.

BONUS TIP – Boo Blues buy on emotion. You'll need to ask questions to get them to open up about their true goal with the purchase you are asking them to make. If this was an unsolicited call, you'll need to create that need by asking questions about people, not objects. For example, if you are selling roof repair don't ask when the last time, they had the roof looked at, ask them how many people live under the roof. Tie the purchase into their life and how it will impact those that they love.

Review the BOTTOM LEFT of the chart to study GEEKY GREENS

What is SalesFu?

THE KEY WORDS

OPEN EMOTION

Giving	Safe	Secure	Fun	Adventure	Happy
Supportive	Trust	Family	Thrill	Excited	Dramatic
Loyal		Dependable	Action		Partnering
BOO BLUES				**RADICAL REDS**	
Helpful	Cautious	Teamwork	Positive	Different	New
*People Oriented				*Benefit Oriented	
*Slower Friendly Pace				* Fast Paced Talkers	
*Softer Tone				*Upbeat Attitude	

INDIRECT GOALS					**DIRECT GOALS**
Analyze	Design Benefits	Logical	Dependable	Traditional	Accountable
Detail Oriented	Specific	Thorough	Results	Important	Prepared
GEEKY GREENS				**BUSINESS BROWNS**	
Reasonable		Data	Market Leader		Competitive
Precise	Recoup	Correct	ROI	Objectives	Opportunity
Fact Based	Careful	Controlled	Win/Win	Established	Responsible
* Research Oriented				* Goal Oriented	
*Slower Speaking		*CLOSED EMOTIION*		*Bottom Line Speakers	
*Monotone				*Direct and to the point- Efficient	

Sales Fu = The Art of Identifying & Capturing Customer energy and using it to Persuade & Influence a purchase decision

In CLOSED EMOTION & INDIRECT GOALS (BOTTOM LEFT)–

GEEKY GREENS

How to Identify the Geeky Green - The GEEKY GREEN is likely to make decisions based on a spreadsheet (**Closed Emotion)** and has a goal in mind; they just won't share it with you **(Indirect Goals),** at least not initially. Did you ever have that customer that wouldn't tell you what they want? Do they play their cards close to their chest? The- "You tell me what you can offer first and then I'll make my decision." type of customer? These customers aren't looking to make new friends, this is a business decision and the numbers are what matters most.

• • •

Famous Geeky Greens – Sherlock Holmes, Bill Gates, David Letterman, Warren Buffett, Bill Belichick.

Tips for working with the Geeky Green - In all my sales traveling adventures I find this one the hardest to identify with. The trick is to find out what the decision-making process is, ask to see the spreadsheet, or ask for a specific goal to meet. If this can be obtained it's possible to frame your product or service so that it fits the criteria and wins the business. The Geeky Green will be happiest when able to justify the purchase with cold hard numbers, and as anyone who has ever taken a statistics class will tell you, there are many ways to present the numbers in a favorable light.

For example, I've spent many years in the mortgage business and I can equally defend the position of the customer who wants to pay off his home free and clear and take out a very short term loan, as well as the customer who wants to take a riskier loan because the monthly payment is less for the first 5 years. There are equal merits for both options, one saves more money in the long run, while one saves more money in the short term. Don't get biased with your situation, your customer may need to save the money in the short term more than he/she needs the money in the long run. People lease cars all the time instead of buying them, it's a similar situation. This personality is also likely to be a heavy shopper with little loyalty, be on your toes.

* * *

Key Words to use with the Geeky Green –

Analyze	Dictate	Logical
Detail Oriented	Specific	Thorough
Reasonable	Numbers	Data
Precise	Recoup	Correct
Fact-Based	Careful	Controlled

Pace and Tone for the Geeky Green – The Geeky Green is a slow talker, but not because they don't have anything to say. This personality type is very thoughtful and purposeful with their speech. The Geeky Green needs more time to think about their words before replying and giving statements. This means that in the ears of the Radical Red salespeople the conversation will sound like it's lagging and salespeople often rush in to fill the void of silence. Take a moment once a Geeky Green stops talking to count to 3 and only then start to talk again. In a lot of cases, the Geeky Green isn't done talking, they are just formulating their next sentence or thought pattern. In light of this, slow your speech pattern down to mirror the pace of this customer. The tone of the Geeky Green is often subdued because these customers don't tend to be emotionally involved. Keep your tone respectful and professional.

How to Brand and Build Trust for the Geeky Green - The Geeky Green is often introverted so ask thoughtful questions to get them to open up. The more this customer talks, the more they will respect, like, and trust you. At the end of the day this customer does not want to make friends with you, though, they want to transact business. The business relationship, in this case, is much stronger than the personal one. Mention your company history and if you have any guarantee, insurance, promise, or any other factor that would reduce the risk of purchase this customer will want to hear about it.

Geeky Green Summary- They are typically fiscally conservative and take time before spending money. These customers are thoughtful and may seem slow to make decisions, but their minds are working overtime while their mouths are shut. These customers are great listeners and are patient but they are not tolerant of mistakes. If you make a promise to Geeky Green, they are likely to write it down and follow up with that promise. Listen twice as much as you talk and give detailed explanations backed up by data if you can.

BONUS TIP – Offer multiple options so that the Geeky Green can fill in their spreadsheet and choose the best option. These customers need to shop and so I suggest you design a plan where all of the shopping takes place with you. Position yourself to answer all the questions and to provide an abundance of information. This customer needs to feel as if they made an informed decision before moving forward.

Review the BOTTOM RIGHT of the chart to study BUSINESS BROWNS

What is SalesFu?

THE KEY WORDS

OPEN EMOTION

Giving	Safe	Secure	Fun	Adventure	Happy
Supportive	Trust	Family	Thrill	Excited	Dramatic
Loyal		Dependable	Action		Partnering
	BOO BLUES			**RADICAL REDS**	
Helpful	Cautious	Teamwork	Positive	Different	New

*People Oriented
*Slower Friendly Pace
*Softer Tone

*Benefit Oriented
* Fast Paced Talkers
*Upbeat Attitude

INDIRECT GOALS / DIRECT GOALS

Analyze	Design Benefits	Logical	Dependable	Traditional	Accountable
Detail Oriented	Specific	Thorough	Results	Important	Prepared
	GEEKY GREENS			**BUSINESS BROWNS**	
Reasonable		Data	Market Leader		Competitive
Precise	Recoup	Correct	ROI	Objectives	Opportunity
Fact Based	Careful	Controlled	Win/Win	Established	Responsible

* Research Oriented
*Slower Speaking
*Monotone

CLOSED EMOTIION

* Goal Oriented
*Bottom Line Speakers
*Direct and to the point- Efficient

Sales Fu = The Art of Identifying & Capturing Customer energy and using it to Persuade & Influence a purchase decision

In CLOSED EMOTION & DIRECT GOALS (BOTTOM RIGHT)–

BUSINESS BROWNS

How to Identify the Business Brown - These clients are often professionals or entrepreneurs with limited time for you on their schedule. They aren't looking for new friends **(Closed Emotion)** and they want to know whether or not you can help them accomplish their mission **(Direct Goals)**. They will be very direct and to the point when asking for quotes or when asking about certain features and will likely have a shortlist of requirements. These customers are used to being in charge and will likely try to dominate the conversation by asking questions and trying to hurry the process along.

Famous Business Browns- Hillary Clinton, Captain Kirk, General Patton, Clarence Thomas, Winston Churchill.

Tips for working with the Business Brown- Convenience and efficiency are often the driving decision factors here. I fall into this category myself; I am extremely busy and I will pay more for a product or service if it's delivered or saves me time. I frequently use Amazon.com because I get to buy whatever I want. I don't have to deal with a salesperson who is trying to sell me something I already want to buy with Amazon.com and I get it delivered to my home as fast as I want to pay for it to get here.

I also use delivery.com to get food delivered because I can't see spending 45 minutes trying to leave the office for lunch, just to get back to the office and only 15 minutes to eat anyway. I eat in 15 minutes and still have the 45 minutes to be more productive than most!

Business Browns all want to be more productive and to accomplish more, so use business words to connect with this customer. Always be prompt and build professional rapport not personal because these customers are all about the bottom line. It's not personal, it's business. They want enough information to make a decision and one common mistake is that these customers are often ready to make a decision long before the salesperson is done giving the presentation. These customers are used to making decisions and often make them without protracted negotiations so check in often to see if they are ready to place the order.

Key Words to use with the Business Brown-

Dependable	Traditional	Accountable
Results-Oriented	Important	Prepared
Market Leader	Organized	Competitive
Return On Investment	Objectives	Opportunity
Win/Win	Established	Responsible

Pace and Tone for the Business Brown- Keep the pace moving along. These customers don't need flowery language and want substance in their conversation. Keep the pace steady and follow a logical flow to the conversation. These customers can get impatient if the conversation drags or if they feel like they already have enough information to make a decision and just want to get on to the next task. Your tone should be confident with few unnecessary pauses and fewer "Ums" and "Ahs".

How to Brand and Build Trust for the Business Brown- These customers want to know what's behind those promises that you are making. If there is a credible company along with money to back up the service, claims, or craftsmanship that you are selling, then this customer may do business with your company. This customer is interested in Business to Business relationships and is likely used to dealing with vendors. Back up your bravado with company kudos otherwise this Business Brown may challenge you and want to speak with your supervisor to deal with someone he considers a peer.

Business Brown Summary- The Business Brown can be bossy and direct. They don't have much emotion when it comes to making a sale, but they do take action out of a sense of honor or obligation. The obligation to family, employees, or colleagues can be a powerful motivating factor. These customers feel an obligation to take care of the people around them but don't waste their time. These are the decision-makers so you are talking to the right person, even if you are selling an impulse only item.

BONUS TIP – Use what I call the Executive Summary and checkboxes off of a To-Do list. These customers love to accomplish goals and nothing says accomplishment like crossing something off of a list. When getting ready to present an offer confirm what items are on this customer's list of requirements. As you go through your presentation cross off items on this list and once you get (very quickly) to the end of your presentation end with something that mentions that you've now crossed everything off of that list, right?

These 4 Personality types are vastly different from each other and, amazingly, each personality type has a different set of comfort KEYWORDS. Salespeople often fall into the RADICAL RED category, outgoing, boisterous, personable, and fun, but that personality type can conflict when up against a GEEKY GREEN. The trick to closing more sales is to learn to adapt your communication style, change your energy and motion so that you identify with the customer and vice versa. The words you use, speed, tone, and messaging will create that moment where you "click" with the customer, and they will believe you "Get them". The crazy thing is that the product, service, or underlying message may be the same for every client, it's just framed for a different perspective.

A quick example here- Let's say you have a Money Back Guarantee on your product, it's the same guarantee for every client, however, it would be explained differently to each personality type.

RADICAL REDS = We have a great NO RISK policy!

BOO BLUES- We've provided a safe way to test the product

GEEKY GREENS- Our Policy offers you a reasonable way to recoup any loss.

BUSINESS BROWNS- Bottom Line, we will do what's right with no questions asked.

Try to identify the next customer you meet and incorporate the Key Words on the Graphic and you'll be amazed at how quickly the rapport is built!

THE KEY WORDS

OPEN EMOTION

Giving	Safe	Secure	Fun	Adventure	Happy
Supportive	Trust	Family	Thrill	Excited	Dramatic
Loyal		Dependable	Action		Partnering
BOO BLUES				**RADICAL REDS**	
Helpful	Cautious	Teamwork	Positive	Different	New

*People Oriented
*Slower Friendly Pace
*Softer Tone

*Benefit Oriented
* Fast Paced Talkers
*Upbeat Attitude

INDIRECT GOALS / DIRECT GOALS

Analyze	Design Benefits	Logical	Dependable	Traditional	Accountable
Detail Oriented	Specific	Thorough	Results	Important	Prepared
GEEKY GREENS				**BUSINESS BROWNS**	
Reasonable		Data	Market Leader		Competitive
Precise	Recoup	Correct	ROI	Objectives	Opportunity
Fact Based	Careful	Controlled	Win/Win	Established	Responsible

* Research Oriented
*Slower Speaking
*Monotone

CLOSED EMOTIION

* Goal Oriented
*Bottom Line Speakers
*Direct and to the point- Efficient

Treat Others the Way <u>THEY</u> Want to be Treated.

STEP 5 ... Connect- Ditch the Duologue.

Within every conversation, there is another conversation- The one you are having with yourself. I'm not talking about self-talk, that's a whole different chapter and definitely important, but what I am talking about is the conversation you have with yourself while your customer is still talking. Your inner dialog.

You know you do it. You zone out while your customer is talking. You zone out while your parents, spouse, siblings, and friends are talking too. You know you do it, everyone does it. You start to have an inner dialogue about what you are about to say in response to whatever gibberish your fellow Duologist is saying right now. It's a terrible habit.

The Duologue happens when 2 people pretend to have a conversation but are just waiting for the other person to stop talking so that they can continue their monologue. You know what a monologue is right? It's a prepared speech that you have memorized or in this case, have at least already started formulating the outline for. In a Duologue you don't have to listen to the other person for the conversation to carry on, you just have to latch onto a few keywords and then you've got to focus on what your response will be. The act of formulating your response takes up so much of your brainpower that you can't focus on what your counterpart is saying. You end up responding in a way that may or may not be relevant. There is an old phrase about humans having 2 ears and 1 mouth, so clearly, we are meant to listen twice as much as we talk. This is twice as relevant in the Sales Business.

I often talk about the Duologue and how not just Salespeople, but people, in general, need to actively listen more and just talk less. This isn't a concept that is new and it's backed up with years of research and quantifiable results. If you are interested, check out a book called "Dialogue and the Art of Thinking Together" by William Isaacs to see an in-depth Academic study of this concept; It will blow your mind. I don't know William but I read his book in college and it made such an impact that 18 years later I still think about it at least once a week.

As a quick side note, I'd like to thank Ron Gordon who was my communications professor at the University of Hawaii, Hilo. He introduced me to this book and without his guidance and dialogue, I would never have made it through the introductory pages. We all need mentors and they often come when we don't expect it. You need a mentor too and I'd be honored if you allowed me to help you. Go to www.thesalesnerds.com and sign up to receive the training, coaching, and mentorship that you deserve.

I know that I have spent 20+ years thinking about these concepts and I could still be a better listener. Being a better listener would help me to become a better mentor, salesperson, father, husband, and friend. I know that people don't spend enough time thinking about and crafting their communication style and it's a shame. People often interpret language in different ways, we can attempt to limit any miscommunication by the act of over-communicating. We want to be able to send the same message in several different formats. This way we are relatively sure that one of the messages will be received correctly.

I believe that greatness comes from true dialogue. Dialogue isn't just a conversation, it's an action that if done right, will enable us to become much more than we are as individuals. Communication inspires us and good dialogue creates more than we could come up with by ourselves. A dialogue enables two or more brains to interact, it's as if the dialogue were the Ethernet cable that allows our brains to link and exponentially increase the computing power. If you assign 2 separate and individual computers the same problem and give them the same rules, software, and hardware they should theoretically complete the task in the same amount of time with the same result. If you connect those computers with dialogue and enable dual processors working in tandem, you'll complete the work in half the time, and depending on the type of problem presented you could have a different outcome.

How boring would Google be if it just searched the information on your computer? How much better would it be if it searched all the computers in your home, office, town, or church? How much better is it actually because it can search just about any database and computer in the world? A dialogue works a little like that, the bigger and more inclusive the dialogue, the better the search results will be.

We often deny ourselves the dialogue, we insist on just waiting our turn to talk instead of listening and using the information provided to add to our network and database. We take turns giving monologues where we say our piece and move on. Duologue is prevalent in business meetings and relationships across the world. We are simply waiting for our turn to deliver our predetermined lines. Take a moment to listen, and then reply with a thoughtfulness that incorporates what you just heard. It's harder than it seems at first, but it gets easier. I'm not perfect at it, but awareness alone will start the process moving forward. Just try every day to get a little better. You will make a difference.

There are some tricks to become a better listener, and at first, they may seem a little counterproductive, but stick with me.

1. Memorize your rebuttals.
2. Anticipate your conversation.
3. Plan where you want to go in the conversation.

Okay, the first thing I want you to do is to memorize all of your rebuttals. This isn't so that you can engage in a Duologue when in a conversation with the customer. It's so you can become comfortable enough in your response that you aren't focused on it. I want you to be so comfortable with your standard response that you can actually listen and then modify your response to fit the situation. If you are so focused on trying to "Say the right thing" you won't be able to listen to the right things. You'll miss the buying signs or repeat a response that is close but doesn't address all of the customer's concerns. You need to be so in tune with your response that you can shift gears on the fly and make it work. Practice your reps so that while in the conversation you can be present.

The next thing you have to do is to play out the conversation in your head. Have the imaginary monologue ahead of time, get it out of the way. Play out the conversation in your mind and learn to anticipate where the objections will arise. If you are ever surprised by an objection, then you skipped this step. Before I ever make a sales call, I think about what objections are likely to come up in the course of the conversation. Often this allows me to think ahead and avoid the objections altogether. I naturally fill in the blanks for the customer to alleviate his fears/objections before he ever has to vocalize them.

Last but not least, you must anticipate where the conversation will go. This will allow your focus to be on what the customer is saying in the heat of the moment and it will increase your confidence. In your subconscious, if you already walked through the steps and have a clear idea of what the outcome of this conversation will be, you are more likely to search for that answer.

● ● ●

In sales, our favorite word is, "Yes", but our second favorite word is, "No." What we want to avoid are the maybes and the folks who just refuse to make a decision. The focus of our calls is always to make progress towards a decision. Sometimes that's an appointment, sometimes it's a purchase order, sometimes it's just getting an answer about whether or not this prospect will even buy, ever. Pay attention to where the counterpart is going. If they are going down the path of, "Send me some information and we'll talk later.", you've listened to lately. If everyone were to actively listen, we would find out that most people want to buy a lot sooner than we ask for the business.

Sometimes your prospect is begging to buy your product, you just miss it. In 2008 my wife and I needed a new car. I say my wife and me but, she was the one that made the decision. She had researched and researched this purchase. My wife is a true Geeky Green at heart. She'll be super friendly on the phone because she thinks friends give friends a great deal, but she takes all the information you give her and plugs it into a detailed Excel spreadsheet and agonizes over the decision for extended periods of time. I love that she does this, I can be sure that any major purchase that she researches is thoroughly vetted, and if my input is needed it's usually refined into a couple of prospects and the determining factors are always well presented.

I digress. In 2009 we were going to buy my wife a new Toyota Prius. We had a 2 door Honda Accord at the time with a baby just arrived and wanted a 4-door vehicle. We have always been concerned about the environment, concerned enough to pay extra in an attempt to preserve our planet. We easily double the recyclables and have at least half as much landfill trash as our neighbors. We've made our mulch, compost pits, and gardens. We've installed solar panels on our homes and buy responsibly packaged and non-toxic cleaning supplies. We were certainly the type of people that would buy an electric/gas hybrid car.

On this particular day, my wife had finally worn me down and convinced me to come home on my lunch break and to pick her up to go buy a new car. We only had 1 car at the time and I was going to take her to the Toyota dealership near my office where we were going to buy the car. No nonsense, she wanted the car, I was going to go buy it. The trouble began almost immediately.

In the rush to get out of the house, she had forgotten her driver's license and her purse. Fine, I had proof of insurance and my driver's license. We wanted the silver one, please, and thank you. Not. The sales rep informed us that we'd need to drive the vehicle first. No sales without a test drive. I didn't want to drive the vehicle since it was going to be my wife's vehicle. I was in a hurry and me driving the car would be pointless, she already knew she wanted the car and I didn't care how it drove. It was a Prius, I'm pretty sure we weren't driving it for the cornering and 0-60 time. I was a new sales manager at a high-pressure mortgage company and I found it hard to leave the office for any amount of time for fear the world would end, let alone several hours just to buy a car.

This sales rep was just on the verge of arguing with me about driving the vehicle. He didn't offer a new solution, try to appease me, or explain why the process was this way, he just wouldn't sell me the car. I'm sure the lot managers of the Toyota Dealership on Frank Lloyd Wright in Scottsdale, AZ have a perfectly fine reason for not selling me that car. I'm pretty sure it had to do with satisfied customers or maybe the hassle of returns from customers who bought something they didn't like. I don't care, though, the inability to get around the test drive and buy what I wanted was infuriating.

I've told that story to thousands of people over the last decade, thousands more now. Before experiencing that phenomenon, I used to hear a phrase about selling a man a blue suit if he wants a blue suit, now I talk about giving a man his Prius. The sales rep at that Toyota store should have listened to my buying signs. If he had read between the lines, he would have realized that I would have paid sticker plus some to get in and out of there in a timely fashion.

He could have delivered the vehicle; he could have rescheduled or explained that this model was temperamental. The sales rep could have indicated that each purchase was tailored and that the Prius was so exclusive that they wouldn't just sell to anyone. He could have pulled me to the said and said, *"Hey man, I get it. I can tell you just want to pay for this and get out of here. How about we do this…… and I'll get you back to your job?"*. Boom. Sold. Whatever solution he would have offered would have worked for me. Arizona is hot no matter what time of year it is and my wife and young child were waiting in the sun.

Instead, I got angry and drove to the next parking lot over and bought 2 Honda's that very afternoon. I bought a Honda Fit, great gas mileage and it still had 4 doors and a brand-new Honda Crosstour. It was new to the market, had great gas mileage, and was more family-friendly than my 2-door number. I didn't test drive either of them and got back in time for the afternoon power hour/ call block. I honked the horn as I drove past the Toyota Dealership.

The sales rep at the Honda location was nails, and I was more than ready to buy. I was going to buy just the Honda Fit which had been my wife's second choice on the Excel Spreadsheet point totals when I noticed the Crosstour in the lobby. Good move getting us inside right away, by the way, people want to be comfortable when they buy. The Honda rep asked if I had seen that model before, which of course I hadn't since it was brand new. It wasn't a wagon and it wasn't a minivan and it was still gas-friendly enough, unlike most SUVs at the time.

We talked a little bit about where I worked, where my wife drove to, and what having 2 cars would do for family freedom and then he asked, *"What if I could show you how to get into that new Crosstour for the same payment you make on your old Honda? Not only that, but I'd also keep you fuel-efficient, more family-friendly (just in case you ever need to swap vehicles) and throw in an extended warranty, roadside assistance, and 3 years of general maintenance because I know you must be busy at work and don't have time for stuff like that right?"*

He didn't even pause after asking me if I'd like the payment. He rolled straight through and by the time I answered a question, it was about whether or not I liked convenient car maintenance and service, which I did. He listened to me and found out my goals on a new vehicle without even asking if I wanted a new vehicle. Everyone wants a new vehicle. Come on, we just don't want to have to pay for it.

The point is this: Listen to your customers. Get them to open up about their situations and you can sell them products or services that make sense for them. It's not the product or service that you are selling, it's the result. You are the solution, not the customer service representative.

Listen so that you can identify and provide solutions to problems that the buyers didn't even know they had.

STEP 6 ... Defusing vs Overcoming Objections

"Closing" sometimes has a negative connotation, primarily because no one likes to be "Sold" except for salespeople. The rest of us don't want to be "Sold" something, we just want to "Buy" a product or service worth having. Sales professionals who consistently find themselves having to use Hard Sell techniques and aggressive closing tactics often have to do so because they have missed the subtle art of building a relationship and finding out what would be the best option for this customer. Customers only say "No" when we haven't given them enough reasons to say "Yes." Luckily, it's fairly easy to avoid objections when it comes time to ask for the business. I've heard this general practice called Objection Mining, Objection Avoidance, I like Objection

Defusing, but mostly it's just called Good Service and getting to know someone. It's called Being Helpful and here is how you do it in 3 steps -

#1 Accept Responsibility

- **Great salespeople defuse the situation, everyone else loses control and places blame.** – In 20 years of sales, I've heard all the excuses. The product is bad, the price is off, the leads are horrible, the time shift or region is terrible, my assistant ate my homework, by dog booked the appointments after lunch, you name it. What I've never heard is a Salesperson who said, "You know what, that customer wants to wait and it's 100% my fault." I get it, it's a defense mechanism, as people we want to deflect failure and pretend that it's outside of our control. It's easier that way. No one said Sales was an easy profession, though, it's like living off the land, we only eat what we kill. Accept that you and your family need and rely on you to make a good living and that you alone are in control of your success. You are in control of every conversation and every buyer's decision.

- **Be responsible for your education.** You are reading this so I'm not going to chastise you about educating yourself, but everyone should read more. I read a book about 5 years ago that nailed this reality and opened my eyes – Larry Winget's "Success is Your Own Damn Fault", check it out. More recently I reviewed a book called Extreme Ownership: How U.S. Navy SEALs Lead and Win – by Jocko Willink and Leif Babin. Both books speak to the success of our will power.

#2 Setup for Success

- **Ask Questions to uncover the objections before they happen.** – Ask about the decision-making process, ask about how they have made decisions in the past. Ask about what criteria are important, ask why, ask, ask, and uncover the "Why". There is an Art to asking questions, the first answer to a "Sales" type question is always the social nicety or what they think they should say, something like *"I'm fine, just looking. I don't need any help."* The second question is typically answered with what they think they should be shopping for, something about a budget, rate, cost, or some feature. The problem is that now we've asked a couple of questions and have absolutely no idea what this customer wants or needs, the third question typically needs to find out why these features would help. The best way to understand the "Why" is to check out the Golden Circle Ted Talk by Simon Sinek. Just search for it, it's a great way to spend 20 minutes.

- **Listen More** – Ask your questions and then shut up. The problem with salespeople is that we love the sound of our voice. Who wouldn't? We have great things to say and we are very persuasive, right? The problem is that we aren't comfortable with silence and we tend to dominate the conversations instead of letting our customers get comfortable in the conversation. Listen twice as much as talking and your customers will like you twice as much as long as you are asking the right questions.

- **Non-Business Relationships** – NBR – CLICK with your Customers, use personality types to bond, read about How to Win Friends and Influence People, study social graces. I don't know a successful salesperson that isn't likable, but I do know a couple of arrogant salespeople who are diligent $30,000aires. You know the type, the sales guy or gal that has no business driving that car or wearing that watch. I'm all for looking the part and those things represent success for many in our business, but if you aren't humble and likable, it will always be a show. Those guys lease the car, you want to own it free and clear, (or at least have the ability to own it free and clear!)

- **Uncover Need** – Throughout your conversation keep notes of what the "Need" is. This person doesn't need to save money, this person needs you to change their life in some way. How can you help?

- **Gather up Benefits** – As you are gathering up the information, you'll have an idea of what the objections will be to making a purchase now. Make a note and stack up reasons why they should move forward anyway. Those reasons are called Benefits.

#3 Defuse the objection

- **Don't be caught off-guard.** – If you get surprised with an objection you failed in the first part of the call.

- **Anticipate the Objection and Frame your Benefit statements to address it.** – If you anticipate a Cost Objection heavily outline the recoup cost and the cost of doing nothing if that's applicable. Talk about the savings. Talk about the long-term savings, talk about the value of time.

- **Use "The Agreement"** – Confirm that your solution addressed the concern in question. "That solves the problem of paying for the program, right?"

- **Turn your customer into a salesman. -** Do this properly and you won't have to overcome objections, the customer will overcome the objections themselves and choose to move forward. Not only will they choose to move forward, but they will become advocates for you to justify their decision.

2 BONUS TIPS –

BONUS TIP #1 – Defusing and Uncovering Objections is NOT the same thing as CREATING Objections. If you suspect that you are going to get a Spousal Objection, don't say "*Hey, so earlier in our conversation you mentioned your spouse wasn't here to help with the decision, maybe you should go home and talk to them and come back next week. I wouldn't want to decide this without my spouse*". Defusing the Objection is about addressing this concern so that the customer CAN move forward today. Remind the customer that there is a guarantee or that they would be accomplishing exactly what their spouse asked them to.

BONUS TIP #2 – We still overcome objections. Don't kid yourself, even if we do a good job of addressing the issues and framing the benefits, sometimes we still need to ask for the business multiple times. Don't use this technique as a way to opt-out of asking for the business a couple of times if that's the right thing to do. Sometimes we have to make it so uncomfortable for a customer to say NO, that they say YES. Often those customers are the ones that call me back and thank me for forcing them to make a decision, they were just too scared for their own good.

Question - Why do good salespeople always appear to have the laydown deals?

Answer – It's because they defuse and address the objection before the customer ever vocalizes it.

Part III … The Brown Belt

SalesFu takes practice. Head to The Dojo.

Welcome to the Dojo and welcome to the Brown Belt stage. Once you hit the Brown Belt level you've learned a lot of new ways to communicate and have some sound sales knowledge. It's all about practicing the Art of SalesFu now. In this section of the book, we talk about some practical tools to get the business. It's up to you to practice the skills. You can visit www.thesalesnerds.com for more information, knowledge, and tips on what to practice.

The Brown Belt indicates that you have enough phone sales skills to be dangerous on the call, but you have to focus to pull it all together. You know why you do what you do, but you can't afford to go on autopilot just yet. You might make it look easy, but practice makes perfect.

STEP 7 … SweatAbility

Invest in Yourself & Improve your "SweatAbility" Factor! This Step gives you a tip about time management and encourages you to be selfish now and then. I encourage you to all draw a personal chart with your own daily/weekly activities in between phone calls this morning, at lunch, or when you get home tonight.

Think about your day and the activities you completed. We all tend to be creatures of habit and in sales, we are often very *reactive* instead of *active*. In our positions, it's easier to **react** to a phone ringing than it is to **actively** make outbound dials and make it ring. We are also creatures of habit in that we tend to approach our sales calls the same way, we all have our standard presentation lines. The truth is that we all have our systems for obtaining and tracking business, right? Every system works a certain percentage of the time. Some systems are just better than others. For example- If all we did was answer the phone and ask for credit cards within the first 30 seconds, that system would work, just not very often.

I propose that we all take action to shake up our systems from time to time. Are you where you want or need to be right now? What action can you take to effect change yourself? I suggest that you think about your business and reinvest in yourself. Spend some time every day improving your sales skill, listening to calls, breaking down your systems, and building them back up. Read some sales books like mine or from different points of view. Not all sales books are equal and some of the best sales books I've read weren't meant to be sales books. Gitomer, Ziglar, and Tracy are all at the library and easily on Amazon and Audible. I read a book a week for an entire year and it did wonders for my career and sales style. Not only did I learn from some of the minds of the greatest salespeople, but I also learned what kind of sales training and coaching I didn't want to do.

Do you want to be a leader? Read some books on the subject from Jack Welch or read articles from Harvard Business Review. To become better than you are now and to maintain long-term success, it's important to be selfish from time to time. Lock yourself in a room for 30 minutes a day and improve your long-term success factor exponentially. I have an Audible account and listen to books on tape while driving. You can also get these audiobooks from most libraries now.

The Equation for Success is your SweatAbility Factor.

Sweat X Ability = Success.

• • •

Sweat refers to your Effort and Willingness to Work Hard. It's easier to increase this factor, just make a few more calls or work more hours. But that isn't very much fun, is it? Eventually, this Factor runs out, we get burned out if we rely on hard work and Sweat to make up for Ability. I have heard the phrase, "Hard work beats Talent when Talent doesn't work." This is true, but only by default. You can do 100 times the low-level activity to achieve success, but this is the lazy way out. It's easier and lazier to keep doing the same activities over and over again. It's easier to keep doing what you've already done. You can increase the frequency and volume of this action, but unless you increase your Ability you'll be capped quickly not to mention, very tired, and possibly burnt out.

Ability refers to your sales skills and how efficiently you perform your job. It's your sales IQ among other things like organizational skills. Most people think that their Ability is capped at the current level, but it's easier to improve your Ability and it takes less time than just working an extra 4 hours every week. Your Ability is just Talent plus a little more Sweat. My challenge to you and the first requirement for being a Brown Belt of SalesFu is that you spend a portion of each day getting a little better than you were the day before.

At this stage in the game, you realize that the difference between an average income in sales and a high-end income in sales is vast. This is the only business I know that rewards 15% more effort with 50% more income. Spend that extra 15% of time improving your sales game and making yourself more marketable, coachable, likable, knowledgeable, and sellable. If you don't, you'll find yourself expendable.

Real talk. You are paid exactly what you are worth in a sales career. Increase your worth and don't ever stop growing. In sales you are only as good as your last day, week, month, and if you are lucky perhaps a quarter. That's it. If you stop selling you stop eating. Sell or starve is the name of the game and you need to stay hungry. You can't get fat and lazy, you must always remain gratefully unsatisfied. Rule #1 at this level is to work hard at getting even better. So many people reach this level and then plateau because they forget to keep learning and self-improving.

Work until your Idols become your Rivals.

STEP 8 ... Sales Mo, Pauses, and the 3 R's

Sales Momentum, what I call the SALES MO, is just like physical momentum. It's easier to keep it going than it is to start from scratch. When I was 17 years old, I went away to college, my family wasn't particularly well off but I had a scholarship and a part-time job. My father bought me an old 1984 Chevy Luv pickup truck and that little truck got me back and forth to more than a few places. I was not particularly mechanically inclined though and had no idea how to fix it when things went wrong. For the better part of a year, the battery was dead and I just dealt with it. The truck was a manual stick shift, so I would just "POP" the clutch to get the motor running.

Sales Mo

If you aren't familiar with the concept of "Popping" the clutch, it basically entails you getting the vehicle moving fast enough to slam the vehicle into 2nd gear and the engine would magically start running. The truck made a few noises when it ran, (we named the truck Gabby because she talked a lot), but it got my friends and me where we needed to go. I learned to park the truck on a hill backed into a spot. This way when it was time to go, I'd just put it in neutral, release the parking brake and wait until I had some speed before putting it into gear to start her up. More than a few times though I'd let a friend borrow Gabby and this friend would find a much "better" spot right in front of our building and would manage to parallel park Gabby.

Now I ask you, have you ever tried to move a truck that won't start-up out of a parallel parking spot? Can you imagine having to push a truck 6 inches forward, stop it completely then crank the wheel and push it 6 inches backward? Not only is it hard to push a truck when the wheels are cranked, but it's almost as hard to stop it once it's going! In those days' bumpers were still for bumping, at least that's what I told myself and the bodybuilder guy who drove that little white Geo Storm.

My point is this- Don't parallel park your prospects. If you block them in with nowhere to go it's awfully hard to get your Sales Mo moving again and there is bound to be a few bumps and scratches along the way. Set yourself up for success and harness the Sales Mo and you won't have to worry about stalling out or getting run over.

Ask questions that give your customer somewhere to go. Don't ask a question that will lead to a "No". When speaking to someone over the phone it's really easy to just hang up and not answer the next call. Everyone has caller I.D. and voicemail. You better believe that a potential customer will press "*D" and delete your next voicemail.

Just like salespeople need to be agreeable, don't set yourself up for a customer to disagree with you. Ask open-ended questions that will lead you in a direction to find a solution, or ask questions that provide positive feedback.

Customer: "I just want to lower my rate." (On a credit card, mortgage, or another loan)

Greenie: "I'm sorry, you already have a 1% rate and that's the best that we offer. Are you interested in anything else?"

or

SalesFu Brown Belt: "Great! So, what I'm hearing is that you want to save money every month, right?"

Which option is going to lead to having a more in-depth conversation about the terms of credit? It's easy to see, but salespeople all over the country are asking questions that lead to a "No" answer right away.

Always be looking for the SALES MO.

Inadvertent Pauses

The second biggest speed bump to Sales Mo is the Inadvertent Pause. Often in a normal speech pattern, we pause to give the other person a chance to chime in and add an idea to the mix. In sales, we must learn to control the conversation. When you pause in the middle of a sales presentation or even while qualifying a customer be prepared for an objection, a request to reschedule, or a request to just email the information (a brush off).

The Inadvertent Pause will kill your sales quota. You must pause with purpose. You must learn to stop speaking only when you are doing so on purpose and it propels the sale forward. When you stop talking from now on it should only be right after you ask a question, unless you want the customer to control the call or just get off the line. What happens when you pause during the conversation? The customer either asks a question, raises a concern, or just brushes you off, and in any of those scenario's you lose control of the call.

We want customers to ask questions, but we have to control them. "Do you have any questions before we move forward?" is a great example of what to do. The customer has the illusion of being in control because they are asking questions and the questions are valuable towards closing the sale. You have to remember that the customer doesn't have a script or call guide on the other end of the line. They don't know how long your usual call goes and they don't know what the normal process is. You need to guide them through this.

I have a pet peeve when listening to sales calls, it's called the dangling benefit. It's when you list a great benefit that helps your client and is of real value, but after stating the benefit you just stop talking. If you pause and the customer doesn't know what to say next, they will think that the natural conclusion to the conversation is now at hand. It's their exit strategy. If you thought, it was your turn to talk and you didn't have anything else to say you'd ask to get off the phone call too. The customer just heard some great information but you didn't prompt them to digest it yet, so they want to do that off the call. Don't put your customer in that situation. Control the call and keep the conversation moving forward. End your statements with a question.

Stop talking only on purpose, unless you want the customer to hang up the phone.

The 3 R's

One of the pitfalls of selling over the phone is that it is easy to get off track. The customer is a Boo Blue or Radical Red and likes to talk about their personal life and the next thing you know, 45 minutes have passed and you are talking about monster trucks nicknamed Medusa. (That happened to me.) Unless you are selling Monster Truck tickets or related items over the phone this probably wasn't in your sales script. Your manager is going to happy about your talk time, but this isn't productive and you don't get paid for nice conversations unless those conversations lead to sales.

How did this happen? Everything was going well until you asked about their job, or commented on their email address or whatever the trigger was. Wouldn't it be nice to know a trick to get back on track? Most salespeople realize that building a little bit of rapport is necessary for some clients, not all mind you. A larger and larger portion of the population would be happier with less human interaction and just want you to get to the business, they already have enough friends. The rest of the population would probably like to know that you are a real person and even though this transaction is over the phone it still has a personal touch.

Ok, here it is – Recognize, Relate, and Return.

Recognize. Notice when a customer has mentioned something personal, something above and beyond the strictly business conversation. They could mention something about retirement, family, a pet, hopes, dreams, a hobby, a favorite song, a favorite sports team, or even a car. These aren't always positive experiences; the customer might be talking about an ill family member or even a death. The trick is to just be listening for this information. It's voluntarily offered at some point by your client.

Relate. After you've picked up that the customer has revealed some personal information it's important to relate in a way that won't sidetrack the conversation. You must control this exchange. You have 1 shot at this and if you mess it up, you'll be on a sidetrack for a long time. You have to personally relate to the information provided and ask 1 controlled question. "I have a dog too! I know that they can require a lot of attention. Is yours an inside or an outside dog?" You must control the question when you stop speaking. Often the personal information provided can be used as a benefit later when it's time to ask for the business. "I'm sorry for your loss. My Aunt lost her husband of 30 years last May and I've seen what she's gone through. I'll do my best to help. Did your spouse usually take care of the finances?"

Return. Get back to the script and the process. Tell the customer. "I can tell we'd have a lot in common if we were sitting over a (beer or a cup of coffee depending on the client) we'd have a lot to go over. For right now I know you are busy and probably want to get this process moved along. What can you tell me about…?" When you acknowledge that you have something in common and then suggest an alternate setting it allows you to build the rapport while still moving the conversation along with Sales Mo.

You have the benefit of asking a question so the customer talks about their scenario. The more they talk, the more they like you. You plant the thought that you are similar and could be friends and that's often enough for the customer to imagine the conversation and start to feel friendly towards you. You pivot back to the sales process and keep things moving along.

Recognize, Relate, Return.

● ● ●

STEP 9 ... My 5 Favorite Closing Techniques

Always be closing, right? If you get to the part of the sale where you pivot from presentation to close and don't have your act together, you are in for a world of hurt. It doesn't matter how much momentum you have or how well you've presented your solution, if you can't, won't or just don't ask for the business you'll get the brush off and someone else will scoop your deal. There are hundreds of closing techniques I've learned and used over the years, but here are five tried and true methods that will get you across the finish line.

As I have mentioned before in the SweatAbility chapter, you must spend 30 minutes a day getting better at your craft. Practice these 5 closes, use one per day, and repeat the cycle for 12 weeks and you'll be a pro.

● ● ●

#1 The Analogy Close

This is a bit of verbiage trickery; it's sometimes called the Story Close and there are entire books dedicated to Selling with a Story. Think of it this way... You are in a UFC match and you start giving jazz hands with your left hand. That's kind of distracting, right? Then while your competitor is distracted you bring a haymaker with your right and win the match. Boom.

An analogy, in this case, is usually a story that is personal to you and likely has nothing to do with your product or service. In the story you must describe 2 scenarios, one must represent your product or service and the other would be the "Bad Guys". At the end of the story, you have to ask the customer what they would choose given that scenario. The Choice MUST be obvious for this to work. Once they choose in the Analogy, they will choose in real life based on that decision. It's simpler than it sounds. Below is my standard 3 Step Analogy Close-

STEP #1   Suspend Belief.

Let the customer know that you are about to deviate from the conversation. "OK, Mr. Customer, I can understand it's a tough choice between us and option XYZ. Before you make your decision, let me tell you a quick story that might help you." Don't skip this step, otherwise, you haven't set the stage properly and your customer will be put off by your random switch of topics.

STEP #2 Tell your story.

Here is Mine- "*I used to go to Honolulu for Business all the time. (I know rough right? But SOMEONE had to do it!) I hate driving in metropolitan areas, though, so the first couple of times I took a cab from the airport to the hotel in Waikiki. The cab company services always estimate that it will cost about $40 to get from the airport to the hotel, but I tell you what, I never once paid $40 for that trip. If I had a bag or trade show supplies with me it always cost extra, if traffic was bad or there was construction I always paid more. If we caught a red light or if it was raining, (who knows), but I never once actually paid $40. It was almost always over $50 by the time I got to where I was going. After doing this for about the 6th time I finally noticed that there was another line for transportation at the airport, it was for the Black Car Service.*"

"*I had never thought about a Black Car Service before, I assumed that those were for executives with much larger Expense Accounts than I had as a Sales Rep., This time, there wasn't a line and I figured I'd at least talk to the gentleman at the podium and see what this was about. Turns out the Black Car service there has standard fees based on the destination. From the Airport to Waikiki was $50 no matter how much luggage I had or what the traffic was like. It was posted and the fee was agreed to ahead of time. Seriously? Could I have been paying the same $50 I had been paying for the Cab ride all this time?*"

I rode in the Black Car that day. It was pretty sweet, there was a TV in the Back and an assortment of Magazines and some refreshments usually bottled water and small snacks. Everything was included in the $50 and the interior was nice and roomy. (The driver was also great and I got his card and only use him when I go to Hawaii now!) I got where I needed to go and the ride was great! So, my point is this… with that brokerage shop the advertised rate and costs can sometimes change and they'll give you good reasons like the traffic is bad or there was a closed-off street but the result is likely to be the same as mine. The Difference is my product/service is like the Black Car services of our industry. We offer excellent service, you have personal relationships with myself and my team, we are like your tour guides and we disclose everything to you upfront. So, if it's likely to be the same cost at the end of the line do you want to take your chances with the Cabbie? Or wouldn't you rather ride the in the Black Car? IF it's the same price what car would you choose?"

STEP #3 Close.

The customer says that they'd take the Black Car and then I say *"GREAT! I'll make sure that we take good care of you and I seriously want you to think of me as your (Product/Service) Tour Guide! I need to ask some questions and put a credit card on file and send some documents to you for review, signature, and return, what credit card did you want to use?"*

A couple of Tips and Tricks-

- Don't use my exact story. Make it your own, just make sure that the outcome is obvious.
- Practice the story a few times. Telling a story isn't natural for everyone.
- Begin with the end in mind. A lot of folks lose their way halfway through the story. If you aren't a great storyteller yet start with a short story. It's typically 2.5 minutes before you stretch the attention of a client. You risk them tuning you out.

Whoever said a picture is worth 1000 words was using the wrong words.

Learn to paint the picture with a story.

#2 The ARC

Demonstrated with the Spousal Objection

Acknowledge, Respond, and Close.

We often hear the spousal objection in the day to day calls, unfortunately, we often lay down when we hear this and schedule an appointment, or worse yet just let the customer ask us for an email and we never call back. When I ask agents about this, the reason typically given is that they identify with the objection. If they were shopping, they think that they'd want to talk to their significant other as well. I'm here to tell you that identifying with an objection isn't the same thing as allowing it to control the call.

STEP #1: Acknowledge and understand.

Before you can Acknowledge, you must understand. Do your homework to understand some likely scenarios. Here is a breakdown of the Spousal Objection in reality-

50% of the time the Spousal Objection is a Complete Smoke Screen Brace yourself… Customers Lie. Customers don't like confrontation and for whatever reason, they know that if they pretend to pass the decision-making process on to someone else who is inaccessible you will give up. You have sales skills and routines; they have customer skills and routines. They have probably run this play many times in the past and it's worked. There is some other option available that the customer hasn't made you aware of or a decision was already made and they are placating you on the phone with zero intentions of ever speaking to you again.

25% of the time the Spousal Objection is a Partial Smoke Screen Brace yourself… Customer Lie. Seriously. Customers need a reason to get off of the phone, but in this case, it's because THEY don't like something and instead of talk about it, they would rather talk to someone who gives them what they want the first time around. This scenario means that the customer has an objection to your cost or service, this is an objection that you could overcome if you only knew about it. The objection that you don't get kills the deal.

25% of the time the Spousal Objection is Real 1 out of 4 Customers that give you the spousal objection aren't capable of deciding on their own. These customers need to speak to their significant other and come to some sort of agreement before they can move forward. These customers need to either get you in touch with their spouse, or they need to become advocates for your service.

Now that you have an idea of where the customer is coming from, you can easily Acknowledge their fear. The objection might be a true objection, or something else, but whatever the case, the fear of moving forward is real and you must respect it. Typical Acknowledgments are

"Thank you, I understand where you are coming from..."

"Perfect, I'm glad you are thinking about this critically..."

"Excellent, If I were you, I'd have some questions too..."

"Right, it's natural to have some concerns at this stage..."

STEP #2: Respond.

Assuming that for 75% of your customers the Spousal Objection is a smokescreen, it may seem silly to address an objection we feel is bogus. We still have to address the stated objection though to get past it to any other objection. The ARC process may take several passes through to get to the heart of the matter.

The Respond step is where you formulate your reasons to say, "Yes." In sales, we have to have more reasons to say "Yes" than the customer has reasons to say "No." Make sure that you used your skills from earlier chapters and have listened to your customer and have some insight into what their pain points are and what might be a benefit to outweigh their need for hesitation right now.

Make sure that your response is clear, to the point, and gives some direction without making your customer wrong. You want to redirect their focus and energy into something positive, you don't want to get into an argument. Your response should offer a solution that makes sense and is easy to implement. Once you have stated your case and offered a solution, you can't stop there. DO NOT BREAK PACE HERE. If you drop an Inadvertent Pause here, your day is done.

STEP #3: Close.

It's vital that after you've provided a solution to the customer's problem or concern you immediately get confirmation that this solution is viable and works.

"I think it's safe to say that we've addressed all of your concerns, now right?"

"Now that we've got that cleared up we can move forward and get you the deal you want, OK?"

"Wouldn't you agree that we've accomplished all of your goals now?"

"Looks like we've cleared the way for delivery now, did you want it X or Y?" (Insert options here to slot close)

ARC SUMMARY.

Acknowledge the Objection, Respond to it, and Close. Example- "I realize it's tough to make this call right now but I believe it's safe to say that we are going to move forward, we just aren't sure whether or not to (insert options here) right?", (wait for the YES, or if it's slow in coming apply a qualifier statement like "because the last thing you want to do is nothing, right?"). Once the customer implies that they will move forward take it to the next level and let them know that you will make the various options available to them and that they can adjust the order as they see fit together. This shifts the decision-making process to the Spouse, which is what they wanted in the first place. Then, re-close and ask for the business.

Your business is different than any other business so it's important to tailor these responses specifically to your industry. I have these responses broken down further by personality types and I'll share this information and how to do this at www.thesalesnerds.com

For the time being get a grasp of the concept. Write down your 2 most common objections below-

1._____

2._____

Now create your ARC responses to these objections.

ARC #1
Acknowledge:

_____

_____

Respond:

_____

_____

_____

Close:

_____

_____

ARC #2
Acknowledge:

_____

_____

Respond:

_____

_____

_____

Close:

_____

_____

A Couple of Tips-

I know that this section is all about closing, but since I brought up the Spousal Objection, I feel obliged to add a few other items here.

1. Avoid the Objection in the first place. Get tacit approval from the spouse upfront: ask if both parties are on the same page, ask if they have already talked about this, ask if they have clearance to make a decision.

2. Uncover the true objection. Use non-threatening language that transfers blame for the non-agreement to the 3rd party, Example- *"If your wife were here right now what would she be concerned about?"*, or use a proactive approach, Example- *"What do you and I need to do so that your husband loves this and thinks that it's his idea?"*. This may draw out the real objection that was hidden, in which case we can address it.

3. Conference Call. Sometimes this Objection is an impasse and we need to revert to plan B, a Conference Call. If you can't get past the gatekeeper, maybe we should ask more aggressively now. If the spouse is just the gatekeeper asks to conference in with the decision-maker, or ask for an alternate number. Let the customer know that they have done a great job of gathering info, explaining the situation, but that the spouse would want to talk to you directly to move forward, it's that important.

● ● ●

4. Schedule an Appointment. When all else fails, move to the appointment. Don't give an inch on this option, it's the last option and you want to leave a wedge in the door so it's open. Ask for a firm appointment time and let the customer know that you'll be setting aside a crucial time since their file is important to you.

5. Even if you believe the Spousal Objection is a Smoke Screen, don't insult the customer by ever attacking their integrity and insist that they are untruthful. Always remain as if the trust has been unbroken. Put a little P.O.P. in your sales. Don't forget about the **P**ower **of P**lease. Remain polite, customers are more likely to move forward with someone who is socially appropriate.

ARC like your sale depends on it.

ARC like you want their business.

ARC because it's the right thing to do.

#3 The Inertia Close (Feel – Felt - Found)

The Feel – Felt - Found technique has been around since my Grandfather was peddling Encyclopedia's door to door. I call it the Inertia Close because once you have started the process it's hard to stop. It also has a way of picking up the Sales Mo and getting it moving again if you messed up your momentum and have hit a roadblock.

I have used this with great success when faced with the *"WAIT"*, *"I'm just fine where I am"*, or *"That's not enough savings to make it worthwhile to go through the process"* type objections. I'll use this whenever a customer says that it's easier to STAY at REST than to go into MOTION. I first ran into it while selling MLM products about 20 years ago myself face to face, but it translates perfectly to the phone.

The only problem with using it today is that anyone who's had any experience in sales will surely recognize the technique so we need to dress it up a little and change the vocabulary. Otherwise, the same system still works today. It's "Old Reliable" in your SalesFu tool belt.

STEP #1 Empathize with the customer (Understand how they *FEEL***).**

First Empathize with the customer but do NOT use the word "FEEL." This first step is similar to the Acknowledge step for the ARC.

Examples-

"I understand why you might have a strong loyalty towards your local/current agent..."

"I can see why you would lean that way..."

"I get why you would tend to stay put..."

STEP #2 Tell them about someone else who was in the same situation (It's OK, some other people *FELT* the same way).

This is a Bandwagon type closing technique.

Examples-

"...and I've seen 100's of customers in your situation with similar hesitations..."

"...and many of my clients don't take action initially because they are scared of making the wrong decision..."

"...and tons of my current and past customers expressed similar concerns at first..."

STEP #3 Explain the solution the other person came up with (The solution they ***FOUND***).

What was the resolution?

Examples-

"…and what we did was find the best program (revisit Benefits) …"

"…and invariably once we take a leap of faith everyone breathes a sigh of relief…"

"…and then we reviewed the warranty protection program and realized that this was the safest course of action…"

STEP #4 CLOSE.

This technique, like all others, only works when you circle back to the CLOSE and ask for the Business again.

Examples-

"So, it's safe to say that we met all of your goals, right?"

"My mother used to tell me to Trust people but to Verify the details. The documents will verify these for you. What credit card do you want to appear on the documents?"

"So, wouldn't you agree that we've now exceeded your expectations?"

A Couple of Tips-

1. Do not say "BUT" it sounds argumentative, instead say "AND".

2. Don't Benefits Dump. A common mistake is talking too much about the Benefits during the "FOUND" response. Make it short, sweet, and to the point. Long rambling responses are hard to follow over the phone. KISS. Keep it Simple Stupid.

3. Practice. If you are using the technique or any sales tool for that matter, don't wing it. Practice this so that it sounds natural. Remember it's your SweatAbility factor that will determine your success.

If you don't ask for the business, your competitor will.

#4 <u>The Buying-Sign Close</u>

Last week I was asked by an up and coming salesperson, *"So, when would I know what Closing technique to use?"*. I dug a little deeper on this question and he wasn't wondering which close to use and how he was really asking a much more fundamental question- **"When do I Close?"**.

It seems that many of us are info/benefit dumping until we hear this line from the customer- *"OK, so what do we do next?"* and then we get the credit card or signed purchase agreement. Now let's be honest, the products or services we are presenting aren't exactly new, right? You probably have some competitor though it pains you to admit it and that competitor at least has a product or service in your same category. The customer isn't giving you that massive buying sign because you didn't ask them to.

In answer to the salesperson's question above I said, "*I close when the conversation gets to the natural end. I prep customers and let them know that if I find a (product or service) that fits their needs I'll ask for their business. Also, I close whenever I hear the 3rd buying sign*". The Buying Sign close takes place by identifying when you've EARNED the right to close. The customer doesn't have a script in front of them, they don't know you haven't gotten to the good stuff yet. Sometimes they just want to buy and they don't need any more reasons to say "Yes." In fact, unless you shut up and take their money you might just talk them out of the sale!

STEP #1 Listen and Identify Buying Signs.

Buying Signs to me are any type of questions from a customer, even objections are buying signs to me. If someone is asking me questions about my product/service it usually means that they intend to BUY, even if it's not from me. IF the customer didn't want to do anything, they wouldn't prolong the conversation with questions. They'd try to get off the phone, elevator or whatever meeting I pinned them down to as quickly as possible, sometimes they don't want to be rude but they still just want to get out of the room. Typical Buying Signs- So do you guys service your own product? Do you use local providers? How long have you been doing this? Can I fax you documents or do I need to mail them? How can I do business with a company or person I've never done business with before?

STEP #2 Track the Buying Signs.

I usually keep an internal count of the buying signs I've heard and depending on how strong they are I typically jump straight to this close after the 3rd buying sign. If the customer asks 3 serious questions about the service or product it's time to ask for the business. Over the phone we usually take notes, I had hash marks in the upper right-hand side of the page. **III** meant it was time to close.

STEP #3 Close.

"I think it's obvious we are going to do something here for you today. While we are figuring out what fits your needs let's agree to something. I've got to jump through a few hoops to get you the best (product or service), *we've got to ask some formality questions, put a credit card* (or billing dept. contact) *on file, and then confirm some more of your information while we tailor this order for you. What's the card number or billing address?"* (Bridge Close works well here, the key is the first 20 words which transition to a close of choice. Don't know about the Bridge Close? Check it out at www.thesalesnerds.com)

STEP #4 Finalize App Details.

After I get the deposit, I verify a few items like contact info and fill out any other details I may have missed earlier. THEN we go back to the structure of the product or service and I typically make a STRONG recommendation. *"So Mr. Customer, no matter what we do today we are going to get something better than your current situation. In my professional opinion I recommend the XYZ for you, it has better features, more for your time, money, ROI or offers peace of mind. I think that's what you were looking for right?"* Or *"I've done enough files of this nature to be considered an expert here so I'm confident that we should move forward. I would like to wait to determine the exact amount of service you need until we have appraised the situation. We typically start with ABC but let's be conservative and say we'll start with X amount of service. Can we start with this amount of service and then adjust it up or down after the test period?"*

When I work a Buying-Sign Close I frame the initial trial as a joint production with lots of feedback from the customer. The least amount of service and the possible need for much more, allow us to adjust things, typically for the better. Since we are happy with the worst-case scenario that means we'll be giving good news through the process and you've started the buying relationship.

A Bonus Tip-

The Strong Recommendation. I first learned this technique many years ago while working at a restaurant in Hawaii. Tourists would come in and they'd often ask about what Wine to order with a particular food. I was 21 and had no palate or experience with wine but I asked a lot of questions of the bartender and people more familiar than I was. I made friends with a Sommelier and asked him how he handles this question. He said he makes a recommendation, backs it up with a few good reasons, and sticks with it like it was the obvious choice. Pretty soon I was expertly recommending the Pacific Rim Riesling because the Sweet Flavor offset the Spicy Asian Fusion, the body was light and didn't weigh down the experience and the acid cleansed the palate for the next bite of flavor.

I soon found that no matter what I recommended, as long as I had a few good reasons for making the recommendation my customers went with my recommendation 90% of the time. The point here is that when we make a strong recommendation and back it up with a few good reasons our customers will listen to us 90% of the time. Sometimes this is called the Law of Authority in Psychology circles so basically people a lot smarter than me also say this is a real thing. By the same token, often someone knows exactly what they want to buy. At the very least let them buy it while keeping the door open to upselling them.

When the man wants to buy a blue suit, sell him a blue suit.

#5 The Integrity Close

This is simple. Ask for the business 1 more time anyway. Everything else has failed. You've listened and you have a good rapport. You have a great solution that genuinely helps your customer. You have used the ARC technique and the customer hasn't budged an inch.

Let the customer know that it would keep you up at night knowing that they hadn't done the right thing yet, or that you hadn't been able to help them out as you should have. Use the Power of Please and ask if they would please let you help them out today. If they still say no, then tell them that you had to try for your peace of mind, they understand right?

The trick here is to be 100% genuine. You've probably lost deals because of a special ran out, an offer changed or the customer's situation changed and they no longer qualify for whatever AMAZING offer you had put together for them. It feels horrible. You get struck with the sudden urge to yell, "I told you so!" but it won't help anyway and even though this deal meant a commission for you, it probably actually meant more for the customer. Guess what? That customer lost out on that amazing deal because you couldn't sell them on moving forward originally. It's your fault. Own up to it and use that experience to craft your own story.

The Integrity Close can be combined to tell the story of a past client that missed out on an opportunity. *"I don't ever want to see that type of loss again and so for me to sleep well at night, I have to ask 1 more time. Will you please let me help you today?"* In my experience, this type of close works 1 out of 20 times. What if you closed 5% more business last year? What if you make 5% more next year simply by asking for the business 1 more time? You'll make this change, right?

Never underestimate the power of 1.

Ask 1 more time.

Call 1 more time.

Reach for and become #1.

Part IV … The Red Belt

Becoming a SalesFu Master

We are almost there. You have the right mindset, the right communication tools. You listen more than you speak and have great techniques to gather up information and gain rapport. You know how to find viable solutions that provide real value. You have practical exercises and the will power to increase your

SweatAbility factor. After you read this book, though, those ideas and principals will fade. It's important to keep up with the commitment to yourself and your career. I find that having a core set of principles that guide my actions is imperative. I also find that the more I refer back to these principals the easier it is for me to teach them to others. I have never met a successful salesperson that wasn't disciplined and had a firm system in place. It's the systems and procedures that create the structure necessary for success.

You need to be a Sales Ninja in today's world to not only compete but to dominate.

10 Commandments of SalesFu –

How to be a #SalesNinja

Do you have all the information and knowledge about your product but still can't close the deal? Do you have a fear of selling because you aren't sure what to do? Are you scared that you might be "That Guy" or "That Girl" that's always trying to sell and is annoying as heck? Are you constantly being told "No", or worse yet, "Maybe"? If you or anyone you know sees a constant up and down cycle to their commission checks, it's because they have lacked a core set of principles to guide their actions.

You MUST learn the 10 Commandments of SalesFu.

I'll go into detail on each. Here they are-

The Sales Ninja

<u>10 Commandments of SalesFu</u>

1. **Be Agreeable**

2. **Power of 1 (More, Step, Goal)**

3. **P.O.P – Power of Please**

4. **Don't Bite the Hand**

5. **Be Honest**

6. **Over Communicate**

7. **No Excuses**

8. **Put it in Writing**

9. **Treat Others the Way <u>THEY</u> Want to be Treated**

10. **Ask for the Business**

#1 Always Agree.

Just do it. Record your conversations and see how often you disagree with a customer. SalesFu is all about taking that negative energy and redirecting to service a positive purpose, like closing the deal. If the customer throws you a verbal right hook, you don't take a verbal swing back and start an argument. You simply step out of the way or duck, then give a gentle nudge to the customer and use their momentum to keep them moving in the direction they wanted. Never argue with a customer, in a worst-case scenario at least agree to disagree.

#2 Power of One.

One More, One Step, One Goal. I'm a huge fan of the Number One. I want to be #1. The Number One also means Unity. It means all forces moving in the same direction. People ask how I'm doing all the time. I always tell them, "I'm doing great! I'm saving the world 1 Sale at a time." and I believe it. Extraordinary people did very ordinary things, they just did them more often and in a specific order under circumstances when most people would have quit. Make a phone call isn't hard or extraordinary, but making that phone call after you've already made 199 that day takes commitment. After you throw in the towel, always do one more. Define the small steps you need to take to achieve a large goal. Focus on the step needed, but never forget about your long-term Goal.

#3 P.O.P. – Power of Please.

People a little POP in your Sales. People forget to be polite these days, I'm not sure why. Being polite has never killed a deal for me, but I've seen plenty of deals crushed because of someone being rude, or being misinterpreted as being rude. Be Self Aware. We don't about this a lot in Sales, but being Self Aware of how you are viewed and interpreted is crucial to success. It makes absolutely no difference if you meant to say something in jest, but it was taken as a biting comment. I once saw an Old Girlfriend after about 4 years and it was a very hot day. She was wearing an all-black outfit and probably wasn't keen on being seen trudging on a college campus with a heavy backpack in the hot Hawaiian humidity. I'm not sure why, but I told her she looked hot. I meant it, she looked like she needed a cold glass of water or a dip in the ocean. I don't think she took it that way. On a side note though because of the power of reciprocity she struggled but eventually said a few nice things about me. I was polite and unintentionally said something nice about her and so she was nice and said some nice things back. This goes for sales too, try to anticipate how the words you are saying will be interpreted and always be polite. People want to buy from people they like.

#4 Don't Bite the Hand.

I hate it when I hear salespeople complaining about customers. It's a sign of personal weakness. It's a sign that you aren't a true sales professional and a sign that you want to place blame instead of accepting responsibility. I've fired salespeople for speaking poorly of the people that pay the bills. Never bite the hand that feeds you. Whether or not a customer buys from you is irrelevant, that person may buy the product or service in the future and it's entirely your fault that you didn't get the deal. Getting a Win isn't that difficult. Even if a customer CAN NOT take advantage of your product or service, you are selling haircuts and you find out the customer is wearing a wig due to Cancer. Can they buy your product? After that customer leaves your store you can complain about why the hell a bald lady was in a hair salon on a busy Saturday, but you should look inside and find an answer. Why was that customer in your store? Was she looking for a friend? Can she be a referral source? Was she looking to find partners to help support a program to make new wigs and get donated hair? Was she looking for a job? Was she just missing her hair and wanted to see the different styles? There was still a way to leave on good terms and there was an opportunity there that you missed. Success is your fault.

#5 Be Honest.

Don't over promise and under deliver. Even though that customer got on board with you if it's a bad experience it will hurt your business in the long run. Be honest with yourself about your product and your service. You have to believe in whatever you do 100% and you can't do that unless you are authentic and honest.

#6 Over Communicate.

People love status updates in today's world. We all have short attention spans heck; I have a pizza tracker. It tells me when my pizza is in the oven, when it's being boxed and when it's on the car for delivery. Thank you, Dominoes. Did I need that info? Nope, for years I've waited patiently for the 35 minutes to pass to get my pizza and it's always gotten there. Update your customers, more than you think you need to, it breeds confidence and familiarity. If someone doesn't want that much communication, they can delete the email or send you to voicemail. It's better to have it and not need it, then need it and not have it. Over Communication will save your deals.

#7 No Excuses.

When you do something wrong, fess up and make it right. You must take responsibility for every single facet of the experience, nothing is excluded. A 3rd party provider drops the ball and the services are interrupted or late. Is that your fault? What if the 3rd party service was selected by your customer because they had a previous business relationship? Is it still your fault? The short answer is YES. You picked the 3rd party vendor and by affiliating yourself you MUST take responsibility for their actions, get another provider if you need to. Even if the customer chose their provider, let's say they wanted their mechanic to install your product, or you are a mortgage broker and your customer chose their title agent, it is still your responsibility to make sure that the product is installed or the money is there.

#8 Put it in Writing.

My mother once told me to "Trust, but Verify." and still holds true today. People want to trust what you say, but they get peace of mind when you put it in writing. I also can't tell you how often something got lost in translation or a trick of the brain and what was agreed to mean something completely different to each party. I once agreed to start a project within 5 days, the customer thought I'd be done in 5 days. Put it in writing and save yourself the trouble. Have you testimonials or a great rating in some magazine? Get it in writing and send it to your customer, have it framed and put on the wall. Seeing it in black and white means something completely different than talking about it to most people.

#9 Treat Others the Way THEY Want to be Treated.

I take a lot of heat for this from some sales professionals. I'm a huge advocate of communication and being self-aware of how that communication is interpreted. I think that the majority of Sales Skills come from proper communication skills. I'm talking about how your message is perceived. I encourage you to mirror your clients, slow down your pace or change the vocabulary you use to talk about a feature. A businessman may want to talk about the ROI of a product while the layperson might just need you to say that the product pays for itself. I want to be guided through the process and I pay extra for convenience, that doesn't mean that I don't respect the buyer who does all their research and wants me to be hands-off. I sell and communicate in a way that is comfortable for our buyer and doesn't impact the authenticity, or the facts about my product or service. It just makes it more palatable.

#10 Ask for the Business.

Come on, you've gone through all the trouble already to get someone interested. Too often salespeople just keep selling until the customer says something like, "So what do we do next?" until they close. They consider that a buying sign and so they will talk about the contract and then put the contract on the table eventually. That isn't selling, though. That's like asking a girl out after she says that if you ask her she will say yes. It's not the same thing. You have to be willing to put the customer in a position to tell you No. You want to get a Yes or a No so you can move on to the next prospect and make a living for yourself. You have invested the energy to learn your craft and get the customer to agree with you and buy into who you are. Use all that sales capital that you've been building up, and Ask for the Business in a very direct and clear-cut manner. *"Listen, Friend, we could probably spend a few more hours swapping stories and me telling you how great our product is, but you probably want to find out for yourself and I'd like to have a reason to come out and visit more often. Let's place an order, (seal the deal, lock in the terms, put down a credit card, sign the contract) so that you can see firsthand what I've been talking about. Are we in Business?"*

How Strong is your SalesFu?

The Sales Ninja

<u>10 Commandments of SalesFu</u>

1.   **Be Agreeable**

2.   **Power of 1 (More, Step, Goal)**

3.   **P.O.P – Power of Please**

4.   **Don't Bite the Hand**

5.   **Be Honest**

6.   **Over Communicate**

7.   **No Excuses**

8.   **Put it in Writing**

9.   **Treat Others the Way <u>THEY</u> Want to be Treated**

10.   **Ask for the Business**

ACKNOWLEDGMENTS…………………..………

I have learned more than I can convey on this page by reading books just like this one. I can't list all the books that I have read over the years, but I am influenced by authors like Jeffrey Gitomer, Grant Cardone, Napoleon Hill, William Isaacs, Zig Ziglar, Jim Sullivan, Brian Tracy, Ryan Stewman, Mark Hunter, Jeb Blount, Anthony Iannarino, Mike Weinberg and Larry Winget. Read more, you won't regret it.

My family has endured several years of hearing about this book and several strong "nudges" from my wife have resulted in its completion. I couldn't have don't this without them. Thank you to Kai and the kids, Team Brennan #1.

Over the years I have had several sales leaders and bosses who have helped me grow in different ways. We didn't always agree on the methods or actions to take but the conversations made me a better salesperson, a more productive teacher, coach, and leader. Thank you, Lally, Apple, Murad, Swims, and Burns.

To become a SalesFu Master and reach your full potential, it can't stop with you. SalesFu Masters must teach the material to fully understand it. Help someone else achieve more and gain more yourself. Everything is Sales.

ABOUT THE AUTHOR...............................

Sundance Brennan is a sales professional and coach with more than 20 years of experience in consumer direct sales. You can read his blog posts, which usually consist of sales rants and book reviews, at www.thesalesnerds.com, Tweet him @salesfumaster or email to sundance@thesalesnerds.com

www.ingramcontent.com/pod-product-compliance
Lightning Source LLC
Chambersburg PA
CBHW050110210326
41519CB00015BA/3902